Cross-Cultural Management (Vol.7)

跨文化管理

第7辑

上海外国语大学国际工商管理学院　主编

经济管理出版社
ECONOMY & MANAGEMENT PUBLISHING HOUSE

目　　录

Contents

中国企业"走出去"与跨文化管理

吴友富 *

【摘要】 随着"一带一路"的推进,越来越多的中国企业"走出去"进行投资、并购和海外经营,成为实现现代企业发展壮大的必然路径。由于企业"走出去"要面临不同的文化环境,迫切需要加强跨文化管理。本文认为了解和熟悉中国和国外在价值观、行为方式、工会组织、宗教信仰、制度、时间观念、生产观念和发展观念等方面的不同是实施跨文化管理的前提条件。

【关键词】 "一带一路"倡议、中国企业"走出去"、跨文化管理

Chinese Enterprises Going Global and Cross – Cultural Management

Youfu Wu

Abstract With the advancement of "One Belt and One Road" Initiative, more and more Chinese enterprises go global to invest, merge and operate overseas, which is necessary to promote the growth and development of modern enterprises. As enterprises going out face different cultural environment, it is urgent to strengthen cross – cultural management. This paper argues that it becomes a prerequisite for the implementation of cross – cultural management to understand and get familiar with difference in values, behavior patterns, trade union, religious beliefs, institutions and regulations, concepts on time, production concepts and development concepts between China and foreign countries.

Key Words "One Belt and One Road" Initiative , Chinese Enterprises Going Global , Cross – Cultural Management

跨文化管理不是一个新鲜事物,其起源于古老的国际贸易往来。早

---

* 吴友富,上海外国语大学前党委书记,教授,博士生导师。

在古埃及人、古希腊人开始海外贸易时,就懂得如何与不同文化背景下的人做生意。在文艺复兴时期,丹麦、英国等一些欧洲国家的商人就建立起商业企业集团,当他们与来自不同文化背景的商人进行贸易时,会对对方的语言、信仰以及生活工作习惯保持敏感以避免发生冲突并顺利开展交易。随着中国"一带一路"的推进,越来越多的企业"走出去"进行投资、并购和海外经营,面临双重文化差异,这就不可避免地涉及企业的跨文化管理问题。

1. 跨文化管理的定义

　　文化与管理密不可分,管理模式因文化不同而不同。文化可以成为竞争的优势,也可以成为劣势。不同的民族、国家或地区具有不同的文化,一些学者先后提出了衡量国家文化差异的理论。克拉克洪(Kluck-hohn)和斯多特贝克(Strodtbeck)提出对人性的看法、对自身与外部自然环境关系的看法、对自身与他人关系的看法、时间观念、空间概念、活动取向六维价值观取向模型。霍夫斯泰德(Hofstede)通过权力距离、个人主义和集体主义、男性化和女性化、不确定性规避、长期取向和短期取向对国家文化之间的差异进行量化。莱恩(H. W. Lane)和迪斯特芬诺(J. J. Distefano)两位加拿大管理学家从人与自然间的关系、人的时间导向性、管理人性观、活动导向性、人际关系导向、空间导向六个维度考察文化差异。冯斯·川普涅尔(Fons Trompenaars)在1993年提出文化架构论,认为国家与民族文化的差异主要体现在普遍主义—特殊主义、个体主义—集体主义、中性—情绪化、关系特定—关系散漫、注重个人成就—注重社会等级、长期—短期导向、人与自然的关系七大维度上。当前,跨文化管理的传统定义集中在跨文化沟通理解上。基于跨文化和管理学视角,笔者把跨文化管理界定为"不同文化背景下的有效管理",核心是对文化差异的有效管理,主体是企业,手段是文化,对象是"走出去"企业所具有不同文化背景的管理者和员工。

2. 企业"走出去"是现代企业发展壮大的必然路径

　　当今,企业"走出去"不再停留在该不该的问题上,而是转向怎样"走出去"进行投资、并购和海外经营。
　　第一,企业"走出去"进一步拓展海外市场和发展空间,从以欧美为主,东盟为辅,拓展至非洲和拉美。博鳌亚洲论坛秘书长龙永图认为,从地域上看,中国的战略开始把发达国家和发展中国家并重。当前中国正在实施的"一带一路"倡议,其本质也是"走出去"战略,带动周边国家和人民实现共赢,具有国际和国内两大战略意义。从企业成长周期来看,当企业成长壮大到一定规模的时候,国内市场也好,资源也好,技术也好,都没有办法满足,必须向外拓展。诺贝尔经济学奖获得者乔治·斯蒂格勒曾说过:"所有美国大企业都是通过某种程度、某种方式的并购成长起来的,几乎没有一家大企业是靠内部扩张成长起来的。"沃尔沃、麦当劳、可口可乐在中国的合作、合资和并购,吉利并购沃尔沃,联想并购IBM全球PC业务都使企业得到发展壮大。

第二,企业"走出去"有助于释放钢铁、水泥等过剩产能,推广高铁和核电等高附加值产品,有利于提升中国的国际形象和展现中国新的竞争力。近几年,过剩产能是热门词汇,但感觉到过剩产能是贬义,其实这是不对的。最近几年国内钢材需求显著下降,导致产能过剩。但是我们也要看到,产能虽然在中国过剩,但在其他国家却不过剩。市场经济的本质就是实现资源的有效配置,把多的调节给少的,把高的调节给低的,所以中国把过剩产能配置到弱的国家,也是对周边国家的一种贡献。

第三,企业"走出去"有助于提升中国产品的品牌形象,打造"中国制造"新品牌。中国是制造业大国,但不是制造业强国,不是品牌强国,怎么办?其中,加快自主研发,提高创新能力是重要前提。但是这个路径需要的时间比较长,而通过买断和引进可以快速提升,节省时间成本。吉利引进沃尔沃,上汽引进荣威、奥迪品牌,不仅提升了中国的品牌形象,也是企业品牌快速提升的路径。

第四,企业"走出去"可以满足我们对资源的需求。中国地大物博,但是在过去的工业化时期消耗了不少资源,在这种情况下,我们必须依靠世界的资源,一些国有企业通过并购海外的资源和能源行业,有力地缓解了资源短缺问题。部分西方国家认为中国在中东、非洲和拉美实施新殖民主义,掠夺资源,这是不对的。非洲和拉美国家资源丰富,我们企业"走出去"通过公开投标等方式公平参与竞争,合理开发利用资源,有利于提高这些国家的资源价值和推动经济发展。

第五,企业"走出去"可以降低人力资源成本、生产资料成本和市场进入成本。国际劳工组织曾经发布的一份全球工资报告显示,2012年越南人均工资是181美元,印度尼西亚是170美元,泰国是357美元,而中国广东是645美元,再加上东南亚国家实施优惠的税收政策,因此广东企业纷纷搬到劳动力价格较为廉价的越南、缅甸和印度尼西亚等周边国家,以降低成本。

经过十几年的发展,中国企业"走出去"经历了在海外设立销售网络,到国企转向海外瞄准石油、矿产等实物资产和参与海外基建项目,再到联想收购 IBM 个人电脑业务、TCL 收购汤姆逊彩电业务等民营企业异军突起,投资领域日益多元化,投资方向从产业链整合转向全球资产配置的阶段。最近几年企业"走出去"的海外并购捷报频传,根据彭博社的数据,在 2016 年第一季度,中资企业海外并购交易金额达 708 亿美元,超过 2015 年全年交易额的一半。在可喜的成绩背后,后期的整合往往是最关键又是最困难的事。美国著名管理学家彼得·德鲁克在《管理的前沿》中指出,企业并购只有在整合上取得成功,才算是一个成功的并购,否则,只是财务上的操纵,这将导致业务和财务上的双重失败。20 世纪80 年代到 90 年代,日本索尼、松下和三菱在美国收购遭受重大损失,其中一个原因就是跨国并购文化整合不力。贝恩管理咨询公司关于企业并购失败的调查显示,全球企业并购的失败案例中,80% 的企业直接或间接与企业并购之后的资源整合和文化整合相关,20% 是发生在并购前期阶段。

2009 年 10 月,德勤的《中国企业并购后文化整合调查报告》显示,尽管并购促进了经济增长,但是 60% 的企业并购没有实现期望的商业价值,其中 2/3 的失败原因是并购后的文化整合不成功。我国企业"走出去"缺乏相关经验,整合方案不够科学,再加上以儒家文化为代表的中国文化与国外文化存在巨大差异,文化整合更是难上加难。企业能否有效实现跨文化管理是企业"走出去"成败的重要影响因素。

3. 企业"走出去"与跨文化管理

企业"走出去"需要进行战略整合、制度整合、文化整合和人员整合。企业合并之后涉及高层领导的调整、组织结构的改变、规章制度和操作规程的重新审定、工作人员的重新评价、定岗和富余人员的去留,从而引起企业文化的改变和新旧冲突。跨文化管理是国际公关的范畴,本部分从跨文化管理的实践谈几个问题。

第一,在价值观上,中国讲求"家国天下"集体主义,先公后私,号召企业员工为企业的发展忘我工作,个人价值在集体中得到发挥。"先天下之忧而忧,后天下之乐而乐"体现在企业管理理念中,就是用整体理念开展企业管理,集体利益高于个人利益,注重员工个人对企业的责任和义务。在人际关系上,突出道德和情感,强调仁、义、礼、智、信的准则,从而协调管理者与员工之间的关系。而西方强调个人主义,追求个人自由,标榜人的独立性,个人权利不可侵犯,组织扁平化和决策民主化成为西方企业管理的一大特点。一家在墨西哥经营的铜管厂的管理层发现,墨西哥工人拿了工资,星期一不上班,星期三上班,事后得知他们的钱没有用完,在工厂工作拿钱享受是他们个人的自由选择。

第二,在行为方式上,中国属于高语境文化,受到儒家思想的影响,讲究含蓄、谦虚、委婉和沉默,喜欢让自己的观点深藏不露,沉默寡言往往让人感到办事稳重、有城府、能成大器,被认为是优点。越南和墨西哥也都属于高语境文化,在讲话时倾向于迂回方式,善于隐瞒真实意图。墨西哥人喜欢穿插故事、谚语和笑话,而不平铺直叙。在越南,人们不舒服或无法表达时通常采用沉默的方式。这样,来自东方文化的人不善于进行沟通与对话,更不善于使用游说来把企业形象推出去。在中国文化中,"游说"被看作是从事政治投机、谋取私利的行为。"沉默是金"在企业履行社会责任上是行不通的,相反企业要对利益相关方披露社会责任和可持续性发展的努力与成绩。在西方,沉默是紧张、尴尬、怀有敌意,他们说话直截了当,不拐弯抹角,谈话直奔主题。

第三,在工会组织上,在中国,工会是企业管理和沟通的重要助手,隶属高层管理,不可与企业管理当局唱反调,主要负责做好安抚、平息矛盾工作,以及丰富员工的业余生活。在国外,工会是独立的机构,不仅有企业内部工会,还有产业工会,他们不会听从于企业管理当局的命令,经常为工人的利益和待遇与管理当局谈判和磋商。海尔并购美泰克受挫和上汽收购韩国双龙汽车失败的一个重要原因是工会的抵制。在越南投资和经营,需要重视工会会员在参与企业管理中的重要角色。在非洲,赞比亚等国家的工会力量很强大,其在独立之前就加入了国际劳工组织,工人享有集体谈判权、同工同酬权和反对歧视的权利。

第四,在宗教信仰上,中国主张无神论,企业管理者的宗教信仰也不会影响他们的领导力,但在南亚国家,没有宗教信仰的管理者的影响力将大打折扣。在这些国家的企业员工认为,没有宗教信仰的管理者无法领导一群有宗教信仰的人。中亚五国的主体民族信奉伊斯兰教,斋月期间无论多大的生意都不能进行。在印度尼西亚同样必须关注当地的伊斯兰教,因此有些企业不得不选择在公司附近修建庙宇,供管理层和工人进行朝拜,解决宗教问题。

第五,在制度上,制度代表着一种规范,是人们行为处事所遵循的基本准则,也是一国文化中不可或缺的一部分。中国的制度形成是自上而下,速度比较快,但易流于形式,刚性不足,大都停留在纸面上,往往出现"上有政策,下有对策"现象。遇到问题的时候,一些企业的管理层和员工会想怎么通过关系、熟人或金钱摆平。在西方,制度形成是自下而上,速度比较慢,每个人都有一定的自主决策权,经过广泛的民主程序,下级可以直接对上级提出质疑,并提供自己的想法与建议,但是形成后是刚性的,对所有人都一视同仁,任何人不可以凌驾于制度之上,具有规范的约束作用。

第六，在时间观念上，无论在欧美还是在中国，守时既是基本原则，也是社会美德。但在阿拉伯国家经常出现不守时的现象，谈判迟到也并不意味着无礼。越南人的时间观念也比较薄弱，约会迟到或完全不露面并不少见。在西班牙，出席正式会议等场合应尽量准时，非正式场合迟到半个小时以内则不会引起不快。墨西哥人认为北美人是不可救药的未来中心者，不现实地认为可以掌握时间，而北美人认为墨西哥人把自己的意志和抱负交给机遇，做事拖拉。在时间线性差异上，美国人在规定时间内集中做一件事情，做完一件再做另一件事，而意大利人、中东人在一段时间内可以做多件事情，随机调整时间安排。

第七，在生产观念上，东方人讲求速度，西方人求精而讲质量，为生存而求精。德国人认为"没有质量的数量是毫无意义的，唯有以质量为基础的数量才是真正意义上的数量"，这样培育了德国精益求精的工匠精神。在人与自然的关系上，分为臣服于自然、主宰自然、与自然和谐相处三种状态。美国和加拿大人认为人可以驾驭自然，通过改变环境去实现自己的目标。很多中东国家的人认为人受制于自然，大自然是不可战胜的，将生活中的很多事情都归咎于宿命。中国人讲究中庸之道，寻求人与自然的和谐相处。类似的还有，在 2004 年东南亚海啸事件上，一部分东南亚人将灾难归结为命运，虽然悲痛，但没有什么可以抱怨；另一部分东南亚人则认为是人类冒犯的结果，是老天爷的报应。而美国人认为人类预测不准确，防范不够，需要发明更科学的仪器或防范措施避免灾难。

第八，在发展观念上，中国以领导为先，企业为先，国家在上，领导在上。而在西方国家，员工在上，社会在上，国家是社会的打工仔，领导是服务角色。因此，西方管理就是管理，作为雇员可以发表个人观点和参与管理；在中国，下属对上司不贸然发言。如中国反腐问题，这是一件大快人心的事情，由国家主导，取得了很大的成绩，而在西方很多是记者揭露，反腐机构跟上，社会和舆论监督，司法机构介入调查。如美国的"水门事件"就是媒体揭露，司法跟上，最后尼克松总统不得不辞职。

4. 结论

企业"走出去"关乎企业的做大做强，是中国经济未来发展的长期战略，而当前的"一带一路"倡议是企业"走出去"的重要平台和途径。企业"走出去"面临双重文化差异，有效的跨文化管理能降低企业"走出去"的成本，培养和积累国际社会对中国企业的信任与理解。鉴于中国和国外的价值观、行为方式、工会组织、宗教信仰、制度、时间观念、生产观念和发展观念不同,"走出去"的企业要重视跨文化管理,致力于结合区域国别建立独特的跨文化管理模式,实现跨文化管理价值在企业"走出去"中的最大化,让中国企业来去自由。

参 考 文 献

苏珊·C. 施奈德,简—路易斯·巴尔索克斯. 2002. 跨文化管理. 石永恒主译. 经济管理出版社:9.

何海燕等. 2009. 战略管理. 北京理工大学出版社:169.

张金杰等. 2009. 中国并购报告. 中国金融出版社.

吴志军. 2001. 企业并购失败的原因分析. 当代财经,(12):65.

郭沛源. 2014. 中企海外投资的"透明度危机". 中外管理,(11):96.

吴友富. 2015. 全球化背景下中国企业海外经营的国际环境比较研究. 复旦大学出版社:63.

菲利普·R. 哈里斯,罗伯特·T. 莫兰. 2002. 跨文化管理教程. 关世杰译. 新华出版社:259.

陈晓萍. 2005. 跨文化管理. 清华大学出版社:29.

Lucke、Kostova 和 Roth 的多元文化论 *

张文洁　范徵　李妍　贾思雪　葛永伟　姚雨婷

【摘要】 以往的双元文化研究侧重于关注个体在一种以上文化的氛围中建立起认知和能力,认为在两种文化影响下长大的个体可能会形成一种双元文化的身份,这种身份可以让他们同时掌握两种文化,每种文化可以在各自的文化身份被激活的条件下使用。多元文化论是多元文化含义系统的内在代表,它对于全球的经理们还有跨国公司而言有着非常重要的启示。本文重点介绍了 Lucke、Kostova 和 Roth 提出的多元文化论,该理论从联结主义的角度出发,提出了文化多元论的认知概念,包含个人的多元化认知内容和架构。基于此,解释了特殊的社会文化经验如何与已经存在的个人认知相互作用,形成不同的文化多元论的模式,并解释了这些模式是如何在特定的社会文化经验中被发展起来的。

【关键词】 文化、社会认知、多元文化论、文化认知

Lucke，Kostova and Roth's Multiculturalism

Wenjie Zhang　Zheng Fan　Yan Li　Sixue Jia
Yongwei Ge　Yuting Yao

Abstract Previous biculturalism research focuses on how individuals develop an understanding and competency in more than one culture. It argues that individuals who have grown up under the influence of two cultures may develop a bicultural identity, which allows them to hold two different cultures that can be accessed based on the activation of each cultural identity. Multiculturalism, the internal representation of multiple cultural meaning systems, has critical implications for global managers and multinational corporations.

　　* 基金项目:国家社会科学重大项目"中国企业走出去跨文化大数据平台建设"(批准号:15ZDA063)、上海外国语大学校级重大科研项目"基于多语种文化数据仓库的无国界管理战略路径研究"(批准号:2013114ZD001)、上海外国语大学校级青年项目"企业文化对服务创新的影响机制探究"(批准号:2015114050)。

Understanding multiculturalism is becoming increasingly important, given that the locations within which MNC activity resides, and the composition of the workforce even within a given location, are more diverse. Building on the connectionism perspective, this study introduced Lucke and other scholars' multiculturalism that incorporates the individual's multicultural cognitive content and structure. Based on that, this study introduced how specific sociocultural experiences interact with existing individual cognitions to form different patterns of multiculturalism. Specifically, this study introduced five stylized patterns and explained how they are developed through specific sociocultural experiences.

Key Words　Culture, Social Cognition, Multiculturalism, Cultural Cognitions

1. 引言

理解文化多元论变得越来越重要,因为各个地域中存在的跨国公司的活动越来越多元化,即便对于某个特定的地域来说,劳动力的组成也变得越来越多元化。跨越文化的界限,在多元化的意义体系中经营已经变得越来越平常(闫放和金兆怀,2013)。理解并处理文化多元化对于跨国公司来说变得特别重要,因为这影响着它们完成一些重要任务的能力,如对公司在全球分散经营的整合、管理经验的跨界线转移、学习不同环境的经验等(Brannen,2004;Fiss & Zajac,2004;Kostova & Roth,2002;Strang,1998)。这样的任务需要做一些显著的文化理解工作和意义架构,这些都只能通过充分了解多元文化系统来完成(Brannen,2004)。有效解决这些挑战的方法有很多,包括利用跨文化团队和跨国界架构单元等。

本文重点介绍 Lucke 等(2014)关于多元文化论的观点,对他们的理论进行编译并详细介绍。该理论聚焦于另一种可以在这种整合任务中起到关键作用的机制,即多元文化的个人。多元文化的个人是指那些理解不止一种社会文化的个人,这使他们在多元化的环境中来理解文化。提出多元文化论的目的是构建一种以认知为基础的多元文化论的解释,以及它的不同模式和在跨国公司背景中的相关启示。

Lucke 等(2014)在研究中提到,当代文化的认知工作(Oyserman & Sorensen,2009;Strauss & Quinn,1997)为文化如何从认知方面代表一个个体提供了非常成熟的解释。这使研究更加明确地聚焦在个体上而不是像以往传统的研究那样把重点放在管理著作上。从认知的角度来讲，文化被理解为一种内在化的精神上的反映，这种反映对于人们每天的交流、理解、沟通和在社会中全方位的运作都有很大的作用（郑石桥和郑卓如，2013）。个体之间的不同在于他们自己用不同的方法组织不同的文化观点、想法和角度（Strauss，2005）。具体来讲，他们用的是一个联结主义的观点，它把认知概念化为不相关的、分散的概念元素，并解释了它们是如何出现、如何使用的，还有它们是如何通过一种动态和灵活的方法形成了有意义的概念（Dawson，2004；Garson，2012；Houghton，2005；Shanks，2005；Smith，1996；Strauss & Quinn，1997）。联结主义的方法不仅帮助他们了解个人的文化认知——内容或者说人们所知道的东西，还帮助他们了解不同认知元素之间的关联——架构，或者说人们在理解环境的时候是如何接近或者使用文化的。它把意象从一组明显的、有特定文化的认知转移到一组复杂的、基于关联和文化多元化的认知。这个理论基础可以让他们在不同的文化内容和架构的结合上去指定不同的文化多元论的模式——区分、整合、包含、收敛和泛化。它同样提供了解释这些模式之间关联的基础，还有完成重要跨国公司任务需要的能力之间的关联，这些重要任务有跨国整合、文化解释、意义构建、翻译和语境重构。

　　Lucke 等（2014）建立的认知角度扩展了二元文化的研究，二元文化研究的是个人如何在一种以上文化的氛围中建立起认知和能力（Brannen & Thomas，2010；Fitzsmmons，Miska & Stahl，2011；Nguyen & Benet‐Martinez，2010；Tadmor，Hong，Chiu & No，2010）。现有的二元文化文献主要基于两个关键的过程——识别和社会化。中心命题是，在两种文化影响下长大的个体可能会形成一种双文化的身份，这种身份可以让他们同时掌握两种文化，每种文化可以在各自的文化身份被激活的条件下使用。考虑到两种文化都是通过早期的社会化进行内化的，这些价值框架和信条都是非常稳定的。Lucke 等（2014）强调多元文化认知，并不是暗示识别或者早期社会化，因为文化可以在之后的生活经验中被学习到。他们希望可以了解到成年人所面对的多文化环境中的关键过程和模式。这并不是说多元文化论不能从幼年的社会化开始分开发展，而是说它有可能出现在成年期，而且这样一种环境可以让他们基于不同的文化冲击，建立多元文化论之间系统差异的理论。并且，该研究所概念化的多元文化论聚焦于认知层面，因此，并没有暗示个人价值体系的变化。对于文化状态，需要采取更加有意识的、像代理机构那样的措施，而不能够像自发的文化身份之间相互转化的那种模式。因此，该研究提出的认知的文化多元论角度可以看作是对于占主导地位的双文化身份的一种补充。特别地,Lucke 等(2014)的方法说明的是与认知发展有关的多元文化思想的问题,这成为了多元文化——文化身份的补充部分(Nguyen & Benet – Martinez, 2010; Tadmor et al. , 2010)。现有的研究都没能对这些明显的理解和识别部分做出区分,并且对于前者是否是后者的先决条件存在争议(Nguyen & Benet – Martinez, 2010; Tadmor et al. , 2010)。

　　Lucke 等(2014)的方法对于那些通过职业生涯获得文化认知的跨国公司经理人来说尤为有用。特别地,他们探究个体之间在多文化认知之间的差异,并且对于不同的社会经历如何导致不同的个人文化认知和架构提出了一些观点,文化架构是指文化是如何在他们的多元文化论的模式下被组织起来的。因此,接触不同的文化含义不仅是现状功能上的差别,还是一种个人独特的认知构建的功能上的差别。换句话说,他们并不认为文化的认知差异在不同时期有明显不同(Hong, Morris, Chiu & Benet – Martinez, 2000),他们指出,在多元文化的思想中,有意识和无意识的认知过程有可能是一个更加普遍的、渗透在经理人日常活动中的文化认知发展(Thomas, 2006, 2010)。事实上,当多种文化在个体的大脑中汇聚并且交错的时候,个体对文化的理解也会发生变化。基于这点,他们讨论不同的多元化模式是如何与重要的多文化技能联系起来的,这种技能决定了跨国公司的经理人在处理公司重要事务时是否有效。理解这种多文化能力是如何形成的,以及它们如何影响个人的技能和完成任务的绩效,为公司培养有用的国际化经理人提供了一个有效的见解。

2. 联结主义框架下的多元文化论

　　在 Lucke 等(2014)的研究中,引入了联结主义的观点。联结主义被很多学科采用,包括认知科学(Bechtel & Abrahamsen, 1991; Dawson, 2004)、认知心理学(Houghton, 2005; Shanks, 2005)、文化人类学(D'Andrade, 1995; Strauss & Quinn, 1997)、社会心理学(Smith, 1996)以及管理学(Hanges, Dorfman, Shteynberg & Btaes, 2006; Hanges, Lord & Dickson, 2000; Peterson & Wood, 2008)。与其他文化认知理论一样,文化联结主义者的角度主要是为了解释文化是如何塑造人们思考的方式,解释人们是如何感知他们的环境,还有感知到他们是谁,并且这一切是如何在他们的大脑中展现出来的。然而,Lucke 等(2014)重点强调精神上的代表性,这种代表性是在一种文化认知的交互构建中被组织起来的。了解文化是如何在大脑中运作、形成思考和行动是研究的基本要求(Hanges et al. , 2000, 2006; Smith, 1996; Strauss & Quinn, 1997)。

　　即便意义体系称不上是文化的精华,但它也是文化的一个非常重要的部分。意义系统帮助人们理解多元化的文化环境,而理解人们是如何内化意义系统的,对于解释文化多元论非常关键。文化研究的主导强调意义系统在一个文化群体成员之间的可共享性,因为他们的社会经历比较相近(Strauss & Quinn,1997)。因此,在国内环境中,一种文化内的成员理解的概念或者活动会比较趋同(Geppert,Williams & Matten,2003;Gibson & Zellmer – Bruhn,2001)。虽然认知理论比较偏向社会层面,但是文化认知理论同样强调个人的重要性,并且是通过观察个人的文化心理表现——文化认知——还有他们是如何形成理解和行动来强调个人的重要性。这是从文化的意义中得出的结论,而文化的意义是在认知和社会经历相互影响的诱导下出现的。

　　一个人对于情境的精神表现包含了一些基本的认知单元,这些认知单元是分散并且有联系的,通过平行进展的机制起作用(Garson,2012;Houghton,2005;Peterson & Wood,2008;Smith,1996)。这些基本单元可以看作是有关联的神经元,只有当这些神经元被一种分布在多个单位的模式激发之后,它才能诱发意义解释。因此,文化的认知是通过交互的认知途径继承并整体激发出来的(Strauss & Quinn,1997)。当认知联系增强时,精神上的表现会出现,这是由于不断重复地接触社会环境造成的。当精神表现变得相对稳定并且被分享之后,它们就组成了文化机制(Bechtel & Abrahamsen,1991;Hanges et al.,2000;Strauss & Quinn,1997)。机制会增加感知的敏捷度、记忆的检索能力、社会内容的百分比,机制同样被用于评估、评价、问题解决等其他任务(Forster & Liberman,2007)。紧密交互在一起的机制是通过平行的过程被一起激发出来的。相似或者相关的概念会有重叠,所以就更加可能被一起处理。相比较而言,不相关的概念,如政治和宗教领袖是没有关联的,因此是被分开使用/激发的(Hanges et al.,2000)。从一个联结主义的角度来看,文化被视为有着这样的机制的一种解释,这种解释是从联系还有认知途径的优势继承下来的,而不是从一种文化意义的混合、全开放式分享的单元集合中继承下来的(D'Andrade,1992;Norman,1982)。文化理解是文化通过最强的联系进行激活而传播的。在一个给定的情境中,想法和行动都依赖于相关概念、自我、动机和其他内在化方面的平行发展。基于强有力机制化认知的理解也许会变得越来越自动,还有更为潜意识。

　　Lucke 等(2014)最先把联结主义框架应用于多元文化论,要区别多元文化的认知内容和架构,这对于理解文化解释来讲至关重要(Hanges et al.,2006)。简单来说,内容是一个人知道的东西,而结构是指这些东西是如何被存取的。多元文化的内容包括一个人不同的文化架构,即他/她所了解的不同的文化,并且展现出多元文化知识的可用性。多元文化架构代表了互联性,还有个人认知中不同文化架构的相关联结优势。它解释了当文化被联结在一起之后,不同的文化是如何被激活的。一些概念是被认知地联结在一起的,一种概念的诱发有可能是另外概念平行处理的结果。相应地,他们把多元文化定义为把多元文化的意义内化了的个人。这些文化意义存在于交互文化架构的精神代表中,这些架构促进多元文化的理解。

　　理解文化多元论同样也需要解释这些文化认知是如何发展起来的。Lucke 等(2014)沿袭了社会文化的角度,认为文化认知是思想和社会经验的组合(Markus & Hamedani,2007;Markus & Kitayama,2010;Meyer & Hollerer,2010;Nisbett,2003;Peterson & Sondergaard,2011)。他们提出,文化感知是社会现象的反映,并且处于或者缠绕在社会环境中(Cerulo,2002;DiMaggio,1997;Peterson & Wood,2008;Sewell,1992;Smith & Collins,2009;Vaughan,2002;Wilson & Clark,2009)。因此,内容和结构都是从社会文化的经验中产生的,还通过嵌入在关系和活动中的文化学习而发生进一步的变化(Bourdieu,2006;Brown & Duguid,1991;Defillippi & Ornstein,2003;Elkjaer,2003;Levinthal & March,1993;Orr,1990;Peterson & Wood,2008;Powell,Koput & Smith‑Doerr,1996;Shanks,2005;Smith & Collins,2009;Strauss & Quinn,1997;Wenger,1998)。文化学习通过人们获取的与不同文化有关的机制(如多元文化的内容),发展出能够联系并且整合它们的认知结构。特别地,像建模这样的社会过程,会直接或者间接地指导经验、奖励适当的文化行为。指导对于文化学习来说特别重要(Gherardi,Nicolini & Odella,1998;Markus & Hamedani,2007;Peterson & Wood,2008;Wood & Bandura,1989)。

　　不同的文化经历造就了不同的经理人,例如,接触外国文化时间的长短,接触文化的不同种类,经历的强度或者本质,这些都会改变他们的认知(Kitayama,Duffy,Kawamura & Larsen,2003)。这会形成显著的多元文化认知的内容和结构,所以个体会由于他们了解其他不同文化的程度、他们理解不同文化的数量以及他们内在组织文化认知的方法而显得不同。这也导致了个体在思考、感知、评价和回应方面会有不同。下一部分我们将阐述几位学者提出的多元文化论中由不同文化经历塑造、相对显著并且稳定的五种模式。

3. 多元文化论的五种模式

　　2014 年, Lucke 等引入多元文化论的五种模式——区分、整合、包容、聚合和泛化(见图 1)。Lucke 等(2014)基于一系列与多元文化认知的内容和结构相关的条件, 从认知角度开发了这些模式。他们具体考察

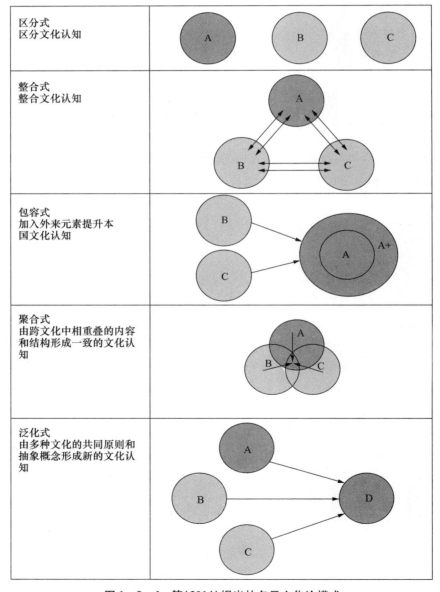

图 1　Lucke 等(2014)提出的多元文化论模式

了当个人面临多元文化时会发生的事情。认知既可以建立在不同文化原始内容的基础上，也可以代表一些出现的混合内容类型。如果原始内容有保存下来的，那么它们既可以被分开使用，也可以联结在一起使用；如果混合型出现，那么它会变成和以往完全不一样的新的认知内容。在一般的案例中，混合的内容代表了一些原始内容的重组，并且可以通过在原始基础上扩展别的文化元素或者通过删减文化至一个常见的核心内容来形成混合文化。在这些条件的基础上，他们提出了五个文化多元论的模式：有两个模式保留了原始文化内容，但是联结方法有区别——区分式和整合式；有两个对原始内容进行了重组——包容式和聚合式；还有一个模式反映了新文化认知的出现——泛化式。

3.1　区分式

在区分式中，个人已经把不同文化中的意义内化了，并且多元文化是被分开保存的，而不是作为一个整合的认知架构保存。区分化的多元文化的精神理解由多组文化机制组成，深入反映了各种文化的知识，该模式被用来在不同文化背景下进行理解、沟通和行动。这里所指的"深入的文化知识"并不是指肤浅的知识，因为个人不仅知道在一种特定文化中行为的传统模式，而且还知道它们潜在的逻辑和动机。文化的机制帮助我们更有效率地理解文化，因为文化机制是建立在与文化相一致的认知途径的基础上的，这种途径是随时间稳定传承下来的，因此会比较无意识和自动化（Ericsson & Towne, 2010）。本文中不同文化机制的集合是独立存在的，并且在任意给定的时间，其精神理解都是由一种文化引导的，而且是由特定的文化线索所诱发的（O'Reilly, 2005）。由于区分式是一种文化之间相互没有联系的模式，所以该模式下的多元文化可以在逻辑矛盾的意义系统之间前后交替，因此可以忽视文化意义之间的冲突（Strauss, 2005）。这与 Berger 和 Luckmann（1966）的想法是一致的，他们认为个体是可以转换世界的，也就是说，个体可以改变他们的社会现实，包括他们的社会和文化上的自我。从类比的角度讲，一个人可以考虑在不同的环境中转换语言。他们在归因方式（Hong, Chui & Kung, 1997；Hong et al. , 2000）、推理和决策方式（Briley, Morris & Simonson, 2000）、自我评价、态度和价值认可（Ross, Xun & Wilson, 2002；Verkuyten & Pouliasi, 2006）等方面都可以发现不同的文化认知，在活跃的文化中都有一种归属的意义（LaFromboise, Coleman & Gerton, 1993）。因此，一个受区分式影响比较大的经理人，从一个国家转移到另一个国家，转换到了一种不同的文化机制，反映了不同的思考和理解的方式。

他们指出，这种模式的前提是个人有去过多个国家的经历，每种经历都是基于某种特定的背景设置,每种文化之间都是相对独立的。每段经历都增加了文化的内容,但并不要求或涉及同时处理多种文化。这种模式的结果就是,个人不会为新获取的文化机制和已经存在的文化认知建立起结构化的联系。当人们处在不同的环境或者人生的不同阶段的时候,就会出现这种模式,个人会把涉及不同社会范围和论述的理解区分开来(Roskos & Christie, 2011; Strauss & Quinn, 1997)。这种模式的可能性依赖于经历的本质,如经历的独特性,经历的时间长度,还有互动的强度。当个人深深沉浸在一种外国文化中并且没有与别的文化群组发生联系时,就比较容易出现这种模式;或者当新的文化环境与已有的有着显著不同时,新的文化认知也不容易与旧的途径发生联系(Strauss,2005)。在高度多元化的并且存在着文化冲突的环境中(如一些世界知名的城市),个人很有可能故意一次去专注于一种文化,而不会去寻找文化之间的关联性。这种类型的例子有:一个在国外工作、专注于东道国事务的经理人,他会主要维护他在东道国的社会活动。他与家里的联系就会受限制,联系程度、频次不那么强烈,而且这种联系并不会和他在东道国的一些活动同时发生。区分不同文化的认知是一种非常自然的机制,人们通过这个可以了解多样性,并且处理一些矛盾。然而,区分开来的多元文化与单一文化是不一样的。他们有可以自己支配的文化意识,这种文化意识在特定的环境下会被激发出来。它们甚至可以激活一些没有关联的机制,并且把不同的文化理解混合到一个合理的综合体中(D'Andrade, 1995)。他们认为区分的文化多元论模式来自对显著不同的文化意义系统的分开学习,并且在这些意义系统之间并不构建任何联系。个人在这些文化之间转移,这些文化是以不同的显著的文化设定为基础的。他们也许可以同时从多于两种的文化中获取这种机制,尽管这需要额外的认知努力,并且这不是自发产生的。

3.2 整合式

在整合的多元文化模式中,个体内化了多种意义系统,并且这些意义系统都是在一个一致的文化机制中联系起来的。整合与区分相似的一点就是,整合也需要对文化环境有一个深入的了解,因为它包含了不同的具体文化的认知。不同的是,整合模式下的多元文化认知是有关联的,而且经常被一起触发(Forster & Liberman, 2007; Higgins, 1990; Strauss & Quinn, 1997)。文化之间的认知联系越强,理解、思考的方式还有行动就会越受到不同文化的连续影响。因此,整合的多元文化并不必然在各个显著的国家之间转换,不过结合了各个文化的部分思维和行动的方式。但是即使区分式和整合式之间存在相似的认知文化内容(例如,它们都有内化的多重意义系统,都能够理解在本地文化环境下的状态,也能理解它们的细微差别、适合性和评价),它们还是非常不同的多元文化模式,因为理解是被不同的认知架构诱发的,只是分别对应于一种或者多种文化而已。除了整合的优势之外,在特定情境中的认知能力同样影响文化的激活。例如,在一个受限制的环境中,当时间有限的情况下,个人有可能不会用多元文化的理解方式(Decoster & Claypool,2004;Forster & Liberman,2007)。类似地,像显著的动机、心情和身份都会影响机制的激发(Forster & Liberman,2007)。

他们指出,文化多元化的整合模式是从以下的学习经历的结合中得出的。首先,对于区分式来讲,高强度地深入接触多个国家的文化机会是必要的。个体通过较强的东道国的文化嵌入和类似参加不同活动的多元化经历来学习文化(Lucke & Roth,2008)。其次,与区分式相比,在整合式中,个人是同时体验不同的文化的。在这种情况下,多元文化的影响在一个设定或者快速的继承下是一致的。例如,个人有很多多元文化的会议,或者经常与来自不同文化的朋友一起参与社交。这样就创造了一种社会空间,这种社会空间有着文化线索,这种文化线索会激发多元文化的感知,并增强文化之间的结构联系。这种联系需要一定的意义形成过程,这个过程会把分散的甚至零星的观点和想法联系起来。为了得到一个稳定的架构,就必须要经常并且重复性地接触各种文化,并且不能只是观察,还需要参与到对应文化的活动中去。对文化意义和文化差异的讨论或解释同样能够促进反馈性的思考过程,领导更加有意识的结构整合。然而,不是所有的文化认知联系都是一样的,这是依赖于经验的,有的联系会比其他联系更加紧密。高度整合的机制会导致自发的、无意识的思考和行为。他们认为,整合的多元文化模式来自对不同文化意义系统的有关联的学习,通过学习,在它们之间建立较强的认知联系。这种整合是通过平行的、重复的、深入的、高强度的多元文化经验来增强的。多元文化的认知是由于理解而被同时激发出来的。

3.3　包容式

包容的文化多元化模式产生在一种被拓展、修改了的文化内容出现之后,这种文化内容在先前占主导地位的文化的基础上,又吸收了其他文化认知的元素。在这种情况下,个人并不会把全部外国文化的意义系统都内化,也不会把它们与主导的文化认知联系在一起。相反地,他们只把一些挑选出来的元素放入原先已有的文化认知中。而且,这是通过将基于其共鸣的新文化的信息与显著并且可理解的认知相匹配得到的(O'Reilly,2005;Smith,1996)。这种匹配取决于新文化和已有文化内容上的相似程度。相似的表述会匹配到已有的种类,因为相关的建构具有相似的认知路径,因此此时就不必改变原先占主导地位的认知结构。新的理解很有可能被加入原先的认知中,因此也扩展了原先的认知。这也是为什么包容式下的个人会产生一种被修改过的情境的文化观点,这导致了了不同的理解方法(Smith,1996)。被改变之后的认知内容为具体的设定提供了更加不同并且复杂的理解。最终,那些和已有的认知完全不共鸣,和原来不一样的意义或者强烈冲突的观点是不会被理解,也不会被整合进去的。

包容的文化多元化模式的产生是由于个人接触多元外国文化的强度较小,但是这构成了一种文化体验,特别是当这种接触很频繁、很反复的时候。这有可能发生在家里,当你和一个外国人交谈的时候,或者在短途旅行中,或者是在国外没有很多文化上的交流的时候。这样的经历只能了解到一些外国文化中的模型行为。一个典型的例子就是,在一个封闭的外派人员的社区中,人与人之间的交流只是基于母国的文化,与东道国的文化基本没有接触。在这样的情况下,对东道国全部的文化意义系统进行内化,甚至对部分进行内化,都是不可能的。然而,人们接触多元文化的强度还是很大的,如在经常举行的跨文化会议中,或者与来自多元背景的同事进行交流沟通的时候。这种学习是通过叙事和讲故事、交谈、作报告、演讲或者书本得到的。跨文化的培训也会促进这种学习,因为这样增加了人们在真实情境下模仿他人的能力,也了解了东道国文化的模型行为(Black & Mendenhall,1990)。他们认为包容的多元文化模式来自对新文化的有限接触,一些来自别的文化的离散的认知元素被加入到了个人原先已有的占主导地位的文化认知中。这是一个单一却被修改过的认知结构。理解会持续强烈地被占主导地位的认知所影响,但也可能适应不一样的理解,因为有新的文化认知元素被加入其中。

3.4　聚合式

聚合的文化多元化模式被定义为从不同文化中提取重叠的相似部分并进行内化的过程。事实上,这种模式汇集了各种文化认知的共有部分中被简化和减少了的内容。文化中的共有子集是通过一个认知匹配机制筛选出来的。新出来的观点在保持共有特点的同时往往忽略一些具体细节(Smith,1996),文化的气质被削减了,具体细节和一些变化被抛弃掉,只有一些共有的、重叠的认知被保留了下来。重叠的认知结构引起了跨文化情境的理解。常见的认知虽然被简化了,并且忽略了细节,但仍然是每种文化的精华部分。聚合的文化多元化模式由于文化内容重叠的多少而不同(从有限的重叠到很大的重叠),也由于不同文化代表的对称性,有的文化占的比重大一些,而另外的则占少量部分。

聚合式发生的时候是指个人接触到更多数量的文化,并且从花费的时间、强度还有广度来说,这种接触的程度是比较温和的。在这种条件下,个人为了处理多元化的情境,就会寻求将情境简单化,同时也不会去深入学习文化,因为深入的学习意味着对于给定的文化更加完整地内化,而不是在与已有的文化兼容的认知元素中选取一个子集。真正参与到东道国的文化设置中需要能学习社会情境,对文化意义的内涵有所识别,并且对它们的激发也要基于一定的提示。这使聚合与包容有所不同,包容式中对于上下文发源的理解关联性很弱。聚合式中,个人的确是学习东道国文化的,只是学的是一个精简过的版本。通过匹配类似概念的认知途径,可以发现一些共有的意义(Garson,2012;Houghton,2005;Shanks,2005)。这种认知过程对于得到一定程度的对文化的理解和调整还是比较高效的,而且不用很深地沉浸到这种文化中去,避免了对比意义的不一致。个人并不会从这种模式出发,但是当他们接触到更多的文化之后,就会采取这种模式。因此,他们认为聚合式是指当人们接触许多文化但是还没有深入学习任何一种文化的时候所采取的一种简化措施。它的结果就是一种被减少了的文化认知子集,这个子集是每种文化都有的,而且还会继续在每种文化中流传下去。这种模式确保了多元文化之间无冲突的文化理解。

3.5　泛化式

泛化式是指对文化意义的内化,还有那些基于原始文化但又和原始文化不同的文化认知的出现。这些新认知反映了规则的抽象性,也反映了更高阶的多重意义系统的原则。泛化在概念上来讲是和之前的模式不一样的,因为之前的都从原始文化中吸收了很多不同的元素,这些原始文化不是被合并在一起,就是被挑选进入了一个连贯的集合。比较而言,泛化是以学习多种文化为基础的,涉及很多新文化内容的产生,这些内容和其他模式的内容相比,会更少关注上下文、范围更广、更加通用。这和文化智力很像,个人的知识是通过文化的元认知被联系在一起的,并且上升到了一个更高的水平,包括文化特性的抽象还有认知资源的聚焦(Thomas,2006,2010)。产生的理解并不以原始文化意义系统存在于任何文化中,但是它们和不同文化都会产生共鸣。这种共鸣存在于认知如何与模式的识别机制起作用,而且是在相似度或者认知的共鸣方面(如理解、思考的方式、影响力等),这样可以发现深层的规则性(D'Andrade,1995;Smith,1996)。当文化认知进行泛化的时候,文化的细节都被忽略了,而文化的共同部分还有首要的理解都被保留了下来(Houghton,2005)。在这里,匹配共鸣的认知过程是发生在跨文化的过程中的,所以才可以理解到一些深刻的见解,而如果没有把这些文化放到一起,那么这些见解是无从得到的。深层的认知结构是基于较强的多文化联系的,这些联系越稳定,就越能够指导决策和行动。

在泛化式发展的时候,文化的多样性经验本身成为了学习的土壤。当个人已经接触到很多文化的时候,泛化就会开始,但是这会产生一些不一致性,因此使一些意义制定的认知简化成为必需。以共鸣为基础的泛化是联结主义模型的内在性质,当不同的文化角度被匹配在一起之后,泛化就会出现。这也是基于来自平行文化世界的相似性(Houghton,2005;McClelland & Rogers,2003;Rogers & McClelland,2004)。例如,Park(2010)指出在面对压力大的生活情境时,容易发生这样的过程,因为与评估还有已有的意义产生了矛盾。接触太多的文化也会面临较大的压力,这会导致个人寻求不同环境之间的可理解性,并且会通过考察共同性和不一致性(Linn & Songer,1991)去了解反映的抽象性,这会导致显著的认知差异(Wenger,1998;Wertsch,Tulviste & Daniels,2005)。结果,一种非文化特性的元认知被创造了出来,这种元认知允许跨环境操作。例子包括一些连续居住在国外并且穿行于不同文化环境的人,或者那些要高强度接触多元文化的经理人。Lucke 等(2014)总结认为泛化的多元化模式是一种简化了的解决办法,在这种模式下,个人要面对大量的文化多元化,并且发展出在多种文化间可以泛化的新的元文化认知。原始文化的认知不再被常规性地保存,或者被用来理解。泛化的文化认知使文化的理解可以在很多不相似的文化环境中进行。

4. 小结

Lucke 等(2014)的核心思想是通过讨论概念化的一些文化认知关联主义术语来形成多元文化论。从这个角度的讨论可以让他们更专注于管理领域中的个体而不是一个特定的文化研究。并且,区别于以前只讨论某个个体(移民、少数民族、移居国外的人)的研究,他们的这篇文章讨论了每一个个体的各种角度。从这个角度出发能够更好地了解多元文化论的核心。这种多角度的研究也能够让他们更全面地学习不同的多元文化论,很有效地解释为什么不同多元化的跨国管理人员适合跨国公司中不同种类的工作。

他们提出了许多有贡献的有关多元文化论的文献。首先,认知方面让他们能够从不同的角度思考全球化的管理方式,管理人员的多文化能力是以不同文化经历为依照的。他们的多文化背景会影响他们的思考方式,理解能力以及行为模式。以此为基础,可以开发一种差异化的方法,用于设计特定的能够促进特定多元文化模式的社会文化体验,由此,他们能够更有效地提高管理人员解决问题的技巧。专注于认知也能够促进个体的世界观,如直接大同主义和全球性思维。这些能使二元文化的文献更加充沛。

　　根据内化意义,提供了一个无须早期社会化的关联主义认知角度的多元文化论。他们的论点是管理人员可以更有效地在多元化环境之中工作,并且不需要改变他们的价值观系统,也不需要改变他们的文化系统或者“表达他们对自己文化的忠实程度”(Nguyen & Benet - Martinez,2010)。这对于当身份和认知不能很好地决定个体的文化能力十分重要。例如,一个意大利裔美国人具有意大利和美国两重身份,但是也可能缺乏对意大利文化的了解和认知。而且,他们提出随着国际化的加深,文化已经不再局限于单一的延伸,或者是他们所谓的二元文化主义。他们向着多元文化主义发展,如统一化,并且这也影响了管理人员完成任务的能力和效率。

　　因为多元文化自身以及多元文化的思维有很多不同的角度,这里有许多有趣的有关多元文化和二元文化的研究方向(Nguyen & Benet - Martinez,2010;Tadmor et al. ,2010)。了解认知如何影响个体和社会化,或者社会化如何影响认知,以及了解个体如何形成独特的多元文化认知是很有用的。他们坚信连接机制为学习个体和行为的相互影响提供了理论依据,但是这仍然需要进一步的综合研究。这可以命题为主导的文化背景会影响融入另外一个特定文化的能力(Benet - Martinez, Leu, Lee & Morris, 2002;Mok & Morris, 2009)。另外非常重要的是,应考虑在哪些情形下文化认同对于思想和行动很要紧,哪些情形下自我的其他部分更为主要。这些都会影响管理人员的个人表现和在一个多文化团队中的表现。

　　这篇文章的主要贡献是讨论不同多元文化的发展方式。他们也意识到先前有一些类似的针对二元文化的研究和分类(Berry, 1997;Birman, 1994; Lafromboise et al. , 1993; Phinney & Devich - Navarro, 1997)。他们的目的是提供理论描述,这样他们能够从理论上理解文化如何影响人的思维和能力。例如,深入研究不同模式是十分有必要的。虽然他们也提供了一些如何发展出这种模式的原因,但这篇文章的主要目的是提供不同模式定义的理论解释。进一步的前情检验,如个人认知的能力、人格素质、组织和文化环境也很重要。另一个未来可以进一步研究的是文化深度理解对多元文化的影响。根据他们的理论,他们提议区分对多元文化深度和广度的理解。同一的和趋同的多元文化论只能在具有共鸣的文化程度下减少广度的认知,而且还能保证有效的深度。为了更好地了解这个议题,他们仍然需要进一步的理论和实践研究。最后,除了精确文化认知(Thomas,2006,2010;Thomas et al.,2008;Thomas & Inkson,2005),文化智商的概念也证明了认知结构和过程与不同的多元文化模式有关联。特别是关联主义可以帮助解释个体思维的内在变化。通过不同的多元文化模式,文化智商可以影响管理人员的多元文化技巧和不同文化间的有效性。

他们也发现了一个重大的研究多元文化模式稳定性和随着时间演变发展的理论机会。例如,文化的数量如何影响多元文化?每一个文化模式是不是只能接受一定数量的文化背景,过多的文化背景会不会导致文化模式的改变?随着学习不同的文化,统一化会不会越来越难达到,或者说当接触到一定数量的文化背景以后,一个人的行为模式会不会改变?怎样的文化背景组合会影响多元文化的模式?一个人的固有文化背景会如何影响一个人在以后进行文化拓展和接触融合其他文化的能力?最后还有一个很有意思的研究就是,一个人的不同文化认知是如何同时发生的。这可能是由于一个人在统一某些文化时保持了其他的文化认知。

新的研究方法促使从认知的角度研究文化和文化模式。这些方法包括框架分析(Benford,1993;Creed,Langstraat & Scully,2002;Fisher,1997;Fiss & Hirsch,2005;Johnston,2002,2005;Johnston & Klandermans,1995;Mclean,1998;Mohr,1998)、广泛共享图标分析(D'Andrade,2005;Quinn,2005;Strauss,2005)、组织研究意义分析(Gephart,1993;Geppert,2003;Gibson & Zellmer - Bruhn,2001)。这些研究方法使用了采访、公共或者私人的文本、名族志学的一些文化分析数据资料。他们都采用了同样的论述。但是,他们都是专注于特定的文化元素,如暗语、文化关键词、推理,还有其他元素。除了文字分析外,这些方法还提供了图表分析(Johnston,2002;Johnston & Klandermans,1995)。将这些方法带入国际商务研究对这个领域的研究学习很有好处。

Lucke 等(2014)的研究对多元文化的认知研究很有帮助。希望未来能有更多这方面的研究成果。这方面的研究也会是对一直强调文化认知表现在跨文化管理组织情景中的重要性的一种回应(Peterson & Wood,2008)。

参 考 文 献

闫放,金兆怀. 2013. 多元文化、企业文化变革与企业绩效作用关系分析. 工业技术经济,(6):91 - 97.

郑石桥,郑卓如. 2013. 核心文化价值观和内部控制执行:一个制度协调理论架构. 会计研究,10:28 - 34.

Bechtel, W. & Abrahamsen, A. A. 1991. *Connectionism and the Mind: An Introduction to Parallel Processing in Networks.* Oxford: Basil Blackwell.

Benet - Martínez, V. , Lee, F. & Leu, J. X. 2006. Biculturalism and cognitive complexity: Expertise in cultural representations. *Journal of Cross - Cultural Psychology*, 37 (4): 386 - 407.

Benford, R. D. 1993. Frame disputes within the nuclear disarma ment movement. *Social Forces*, 71(3): 677 - 701.

Berger, P. L. & Luckmann, T. 1966. *The Social Construction of Reality: A Treatise in the Sociology of Knowledge.* Garden City, NY: Doubleday.

Berry, J. W. 1997. Immigration, acculturation, and adaptation. *Applied Psychology*, 46 (1): 5 - 34.

Birman, D. 1994. Acculturation and human diversity in a multi - cultural society. In E. J. Trickett, R. J. Watts & D. Birman (Eds), *Human Diversity: Perspectives on People in Context.* San Francisco, CA: Jossey - Bass.

Black, J. S. & Mendenhall, M. 1990. Cross - cultural training effectiveness: A review and a theoretical framework for future research. *Academy of Management Review*, 15 (1): 113 - 136.

Bourdieu, P. [1977] 2006. *Outline of a Theory of Practice.* Cambridge: Cambridge University Press.

Brannen, M. Y. 2004. When Mickey loses face: Recontextuali zation, semantic fit, and the semiotics of foreignness. *Academy of Management Review*, 29(4): 593 - 616.

Brannen, M. Y. & Thomas, D. C. 2010. Bicultural individuals in organizations: Implications and opportunity. *International Journal of Cross Cultural Management*, 10 (1): 5 - 16.

Briley, D. A. , Morris, M. W. & Simonson, I. 2000. Reasons as carriers of culture: Dynamic versus dispositional models of cultural influence on decision making. *Journal of Consumer Research*, 27(2): 157 - 178.

Cerulo, K. A. (Ed) 2002. Establishing a sociology of culture and cognition. In, *Culture in Mind: Toward a Sociology of Culture and Cognition.* New York: Routledge.

Creed, W. E. D. , Langstraat, J. A. & Scully, M. A. 2002. A picture of the frame: Frame analysis as technique and as politics. *Organizational Research Methods*, 5 (1): 34 - 55.

D'Andrade, R. 1992. Schemas and motivation. In R. D'Andrade & C. Strauss (Eds), *Human Motives and Cultural Models.* Cambridge: Cambridge University Press.

D'Andrade, R. G. 1995. *The Development of Cognitive Anthropology.* Cambridge: Cambridge University Press.

D'Andrade, R. 2005. Some methods for studying cultural cogni tive structures. In N.

Quinn (Ed), *Finding Culture in Talk*. New York: Palgrave Macmillan.

Dawson, M. R. W. 2004. *Minds and Machines: Connectionism and Psychological Modeling*. Oxford: Blackwell Publishing.

Decoster, J. & Claypool, H. M. 2004. A meta – analysis of priming effects on impression formation supporting a general model of informational biases. *Personality and Social Psychology Review*, 8(1): 2 – 27.

DeFillippi, R. & Ornstein, S. 2003. Psychological perspectives underlying theories of organizational learning. In M. Easterby – Smith & M. A. Lyles (Eds), *The Blackwell Handbook of Organizational Learning and Knowledge Management*. Oxford: Blackwell.

DiMaggio, P. J. 1997. Culture and cognition. *Annual Review of Sociology*, 23(1): 263 – 287.

Elkjaer, B. 2003. Social learning theory: Learning as participation in social processes. In M. Easterby – Smith & M. A. Lyles (Eds), *The Blackwell Handbook of Organizational Learning and Knowledge Management*. Oxford: Blackwell.

Ericsson, K. A. & Towne, T. J. 2010. Expertise. *Wiley Interdisciplinary Reviews: Cognitive Science*, 1(4): 404 – 416.

Fisher, K. D. 1997. Locating frames in the discursive universe. *Sociological Research Online*, 2(3): http://socresonline. org. uk/2/ 3/4. html.

Fiss, P. C. & Hirsch, P. M. 2005. The discourse of globalization: Framing and sensemaking of an emerging concept. *American Sociological Review*, 70(1): 29 – 52.

Fiss, P. C. & Zajac, E. J. 2004. The diffusion of ideas over contested terrain: The (non)adoption of a shareholder value orientation among German firms. *Administrative Science Quarterly*, 49(4): 501 – 534.

Förster, J. & Liberman, N. 2007. Knowledge activation. In E. T. Higgins & A. Kruglanski (Eds), *Social Psychology: Handbook of Basic Principles*. New York: Guilford.

Garson, J. 2012. Connectionism. In E. N. Zalta (Ed), *The Stanford Encyclopedia of Philosophy*. http://plato. stanford. edu/archives/ win2012/entries/connectionism/ (Winter 2012 Edition).

Gephart, Jr. , R. P. 1993. The textual approach: Risk and blame in disaster sensemaking. *Academy of Management Journal*, 36(6): 1465 – 1515.

Geppert, M. 2003. Sensemaking and politics in MNCs: A com parative analysis of vocabularies within the global manufacturing discourse in one industrial sector. *Journal of Management Inquiry*, 12(4): 312 – 329.

Geppert, M. , Williams, K. & Matten, D. 2003. The social construction of contextual rationalities in MNCs: An Anglo – German comparison of subsidiary choice. *The Journal of Management Studies*, 40(3): 617 – 641.

Gherardi, S. , Nicolini, D. & Odella, F. 1998. Toward a social understanding of how people learn in organizations: The notion of situated curriculum. *Management Learning*, 29(3): 273 – 297.

Green, S. E. 2004. A rhetorical theory of diffusion. *Academy of Management Review*, 29(4): 653 – 669.

Hanges, P. J., Lord, R. & Dickson, M. 2000. An information – processing perspective on leadership and culture: A case for connectionist architecture. *Applied Psychology: An International Review*, 49(1): 133 – 161.

Higgins, E. T. 1990. Personality, social psychology, and person – situation relations: Standards and knowledge activation as a common language. In L. A. Pervin (Ed), *Handbook of Personality: Theory and Research*. New York: Guilford.

Hong, Y. Y., Chiu, C. Y. & Kung, M. 1997. Bringing culture out in front: Effects of cultural meaning system activation on social cognition. In K. Leung, Y. Kashima, U. Kim & S. Yamaguchi (Eds), *Progress in Asian Social Psychology*, Vol. 1, Singapore: Wiley.

Hong, Y., Morris, M., Chiu, C. & Benet – Martínez, V. 2000. Multicultural minds: A dynamic constructivist approach to culture and cognition. *American Psychologist*, 55(7): 709 – 720.

Houghton, G. 2005. *Connectionist models in cognitive psychology*. Hove: Psychology Press.

Johnston, H. 2002. Verification and proof in frame and discourse analysis. In B. Klandermans & S. Staggenborg (Eds), *Methods of Social Movement Research*. Minneapolis, MN: University of Minnesota Press.

Johnston, H. 2005. Comparative frame analysis. In H. Johnston & J. A. Noakes (Eds), *Frames of Protest: Social Movements and the Framing Perspective*. Lanham, MD: Rowman & Littlefield.

Johnston, H. & Klandermans, B. (Eds) 1995. The cultural analysis of social movements. In, *Social movements and Culture*. Minneapolis, MN: University of Minnesota Press.

Kitayama, S., Duffy, S., Kawamura, T. & Larsen, J. T. 2003. Perceiving an object and its context in different cultures. *Psychological Science*, 14(3): 201 – 206.

Kostova, T. & Roth, K. 2002. Adoption of an organizational practice by subsidiaries of multinational corporations: Institutional and relational effects. *Academy of Management Journal*, 45(1): 215 – 233.

LaFromboise, T., Coleman, H. L. K. & Gerton, J. 1993. Psychological impact of biculturalism: Evidence and theory. *Psychological Bulletin*, 114(3): 395 – 412.

Levinthal, D. & March, J. 1993. The myopia of learning. *Strategic Management Journal*, 14(8): 95 – 112.

Linn, M. C. & Songer, N. B. 1991. Cognitive and conceptual change in adolescence. *American Journal of Education*, 99(4): 379 – 417.

Lücke, G. & Roth, K. 2008. An embeddedness view of biculturalism. Working Paper D – 08 – 07, *South Carolina CIBER Working Paper Series*.

Lücke, G. , Kostova, T. & Roth, K. (2014). Multiculturalism from a cognitive perspective: Patterns and implications. *Journal of International Business Studies*, 45(2), 169 – 190.

Markus, H. R. & Hamedani, M. G. 2007. Sociocultural psychology: The dynamic interdependence among self systems and social systems. In S. Kitayama & D. Cohen (Eds), *Handbook of Cultural Psychology*. New York: Guilford.

Markus, H. R. & Kitayama, S. 2010. Cultures and selves: A cycle of mutual constitution. *Perspectives on Psychological Science*, 5(4): 420 – 430.

McClelland, J. L. & Rogers, T. T. 2003. The parallel distributed processing approach to semantic cognition. *Nature Reviews Neuroscience*, 4(4): 310 – 322.

McLean, P. D. 1998. A frame analysis of favor seeking in the renaissance: Agency, networks, and political culture. *American Journal of Sociology*, 104(1): 51 – 91.

Mohr, J. W. 1998. Measuring meaning structures. *Annual Review of Sociology*, 24(1): 345 – 370.

Nisbett, R. E. 2003. *The Geography of Thought: How Asians and Westerners Think Differently, and Why*. New York: Free Press.

Norman, D. A. 1982. *Learning and Memory*. San Francisco: Freeman.

Orr, J. E. 1990. Sharing knowledge, celebrating identity: Community memory in a service culture. In D. Middleton & D. Edwards (Eds), *Collective Remembering: Memory in Society*. Beverly Hills, CA: Sage.

Oyserman, D. & Sorensen, N. 2009. Understanding cultural syndrome effects on what and how we think: A situated cognition model. In R. Wyer, Y. Y. Hong & C. Y. Chiu (Eds), *Understanding Culture: Theory, Research and Application*. New York: Psychology Press.

Park, C. L. 2010. Making sense of the meaning literature: An integrative review of meaning making and its effects on adjustment to stressful life events. *Psychological Bulletin*, 136(2): 257 – 301.

Peterson, M. F. & Søndergaard, M. 2011. Traditions and transitions in quantitative societal culture research in organization studies. *Organization Studies*, 32 (11): 1539 – 1558.

Phinney, J. S. & Devich – Navarro, M. 1997. Variations in bicultural identification among African American and Mexican American adolescents. *Journal of Research on Adolescence*, 7(1): 3 – 32.

Powell, W. W. , Koput, K. W. & Smith – Doerr, L. 1996. Interorga nizational collaboration and the locus of innovation: Networks of learning in biotechnology. *Administrative Science Quarterly*, 41(1): 116 – 145.

Quinn, N. (Eds) 2005. How to reconstruct schemas people share, from what they say.

In, *Finding Culture in Talk*. New York: Palgrave Macmillan.

Rogers, T. T. & McClelland, J. L. 2004. *Semantic Cognition: A Parallel Distributed Processing Approach*. Cambridge, MA: MIT Press.

Roskos, K. A. & Christie, J. F. 2011. Mindbrain and play – literacy connections. *Journal of Early Childhood Literacy*, 11(1): 73 – 94.

Sewell, Jr. , W. H. 1992. A theory of structure: Duality, agency, and transformation. *American Journal of Sociology*, 98(1): 1 – 29.

Shanks, D. R. 2005. Connectionist models of basic human learning processes. In G. Houghton (Ed), *Connectionist Models in Cognitive Psychology*. Hove: Psychology Press.

Smith, E. R. 1996. What do connectionism and social psychology offer each other? *Journal of Personality and Social Psychology*, 70(5): 893 – 912.

Smith, E. R. & Collins, E. C. 2009. Contextualizing person perception: Distributed social cognition. *Psychological Review*, 116(2): 343 – 364.

Strauss, C. 2005. Analyzing discourse for cultural complexity. In N. Quinn (Ed), *Finding Culture in Talk*. New York: Palgrave Macmillan.

Strauss, C. & Quinn, N. 1997. *A Cognitive Theory of Cultural Meaning*. Cambridge: Cambridge University Press.

Tadmor, C. T. & Tetlock, P. E. 2006. Biculturalism: A model of the effects of second – culture exposure on acculturation and integrative complexity. *Journal of Cross – Cultural Psychology*, 37 (2): 173 – 190.

Thomas, D. C. 2006. Domain and development of cultural intelligence: The importance of mindfulness. *Group & Organization Management*, 31(1): 78 – 99.

Thomas, D. C. 2010. Cultural intelligence and all that jazz: A cognitive revolution in international management research? In T. Devinney, T. Pedersen & L. Tihanyi (Eds), *The Past, Present and Future of International Business & Management*. Bingley: Emerald.

Thomas, D. C. & Inkson, K. 2005. Cultural intelligence. *Consulting to Management*, 16 (1): 5 – 9.

Thomas, D. C. et al. 2008. Cultural intelligence: Domain and assessment. *International Journal of Cross Cultural Management*, 8(2): 123 – 143.

Vaughan, D. 2002. Signals and interpretive work: The role of culture in a theory of practical action. In K. Cerulo (Ed), *Culture in Mind: Toward a Sociology of Culture and Cognition*. New York: Routledge.

Verkuyten, M. & Pouliasi, K. 2006. Biculturalism and group identification: The mediating role of identification in cultural frame switching. *Journal of Cross – Cultural Psychology*, 37(3): 312 – 326.

Wenger, E. 1998. *Communities of Practice: Learning, Meaning, and Identity*. Cambridge: Cambridge University Press.

Wertsch, J. V. , Tulviste, P. & Daniels, H. 2005. L. S. *Vygotsky and Contemporary Developmental Psychology.* London: Routledge.

Wilson, R. A. & Clark, A. 2009. How to situate cognition: Letting nature take its course. In M. Aydede & P. Robbins (Eds), *The Cambridge Handbook of Situated Cognition.* Cambridge: Cambridge University Press.

Wood, R. E. & Bandura, A. 1989. Social cognitive theory of organizational management. *Academy of Management Review*, 14(3): 361 – 384.

Foreign Market Knowledge, Country Sales Breadth and Innovative Performance of Emerging Economy Firms

Jiqing Zhu [*]

Abstract We investigate how the internationalization of firms from an emerging economy influences the innovative performance of those firms. While it is widely acknowledged that innovation is vital for firms in emerging economies seeking to "catch – up", there are competing views on the role played by internationalization on such firms' ability to develop new products, file patents, and gain sales from new products. We address this issue by examining how the relationship between foreign market knowledge and innovative performance in emerging economy firms is moderated by country sales breadth, i. e., the diversity of countries in which the firm derives sales. We test two competing theoretical perspectives on this relationship: diversity logic suggesting country sales breadth is beneficial to innovative performance, and time compression diseconomies logic suggesting the opposite. Drawing from a sample of 92 Chinese firms, we show that foreign market knowledge has a positive impact on innovative performance, and that this relationship is positively moderated by country sales breadth. The findings also indicate interesting non – linear effects, firstly of a U – shaped relationship between foreign market knowledge and innovative performance, and secondly of a negative interaction between country sales breadth and the quadratic term for foreign market knowledge on perceptions of satisfaction with patenting. While our study provides support for a theory of innovation in emerging economy firms based on learning from diversity in foreign markets, there is evidence that time compression diseconomies also matter on a smaller scale. Our study suggests that managers in Chinese new ventures have developed effective capabilities in accessing, integrating and utilizing foreign market knowledge from a breadth of international sources in their quest for innovation.

Key Words Innovative Performance, Foreign Market Knowledge, Internationalization, China

* Jiqing Zhu is professor at School of Business and Management, Shanghai International Studies University, China.

海外市场知识、国家销售范围与
新兴经济体企业的创新绩效

朱吉庆

【摘要】　本文研究新兴经济体的企业国际化是如何影响其创新绩效的。尽管大多数研究都认为,创新对寻求赶超的新兴经济体的企业是至关重要的,然而,对于国际化在其新产品开发、专利、新产品销售等方面的能力中所起的作用,却有着不同的观点。本文研究的是新兴经济体企业的海外市场知识与创新绩效是如何受到国家销售范围(诸如产品销往国家的多样性)调节的。我们试图检验在这一关系上的两种相互竞争的理论视角:多样化逻辑认为国家销售范围有助于创新绩效,而时间压缩的非经济性逻辑则认为相反。基于中国 92 家企业的样本,我们认为海外市场知识对创新绩效有着正向的影响,这种关系受到国家销售范围的正向调节。研究发现了非线性关系的存在,首先,海外市场知识与创新绩效之间存在 U 形关系;其次,国家销售范围与海外市场知识的二次方存在负向的互动关系。尽管本文的研究为新兴经济体企业的创新基于海外市场学习提供了理论支持,但仍有证据表明,时间压缩的非经济性在小规模上也起着一定的作用。我们的研究表明,中国新创企业的管理人员已经具备了有效的从一定范围的国际市场整合和应用海外市场知识以满足创新需求的能力。

【关键词】　创新绩效、海外市场知识、国际化、中国

1. Introduction

Accumulation of new market knowledge is one of the main benefits for firms operating in international markets (Cantwell & Piscitello, 2000; Kuemmerle, 1999). While early studies saw foreign expansion as a gradual process of knowledge accumulation (Johanson & Vahlne, 1977), scholars more recently have shown how firms can rapidly internationalize through networks (Johanson & Vahlne, 2009) and expand into multiple countries in a short space of time (Knight & Cavusgil, 2004). Rapid international expansion, however, can be detrimental to a firm's performance if it is not able to effectively coordinate its experiences (Barkema, Bell & Pennings, 1996a; Gaur & Lu, 2007; Makino & Delios, 1996). Indeed, the firm may draw erroneous inferences and learn incorrectly from early expansions when new to dissimilar circumstances (Makino & Delios, 1996; Zeng, Shenkar, Lee & Song, 2013).

This potential hazard of internationalizing is particularly relevant to firms from emerging economies that seek not only sales growth in new markets but also market knowledge that will help them in their drive to be more innovative[1]. These so – called late – comer firms are under pressure to develop innovative capabilities as their economy seeks to "catch – up" and compete with firms from developed economies (Guan, Mok, Yam, Chin & Pun, 2006; Kumaraswamy, Mudambi, Saranga & Tripathy, 2012; Luo & Tung, 2007; Sim & Pandian, 2003). Scholars have noted how emerging economy firms are faced with a number of conditions that challenge their ability to catch – up. Firstly, they more likely to start from a position of technological backwardness than developed economy firms and are faced with two fundamental choices: ①to remain in a state of technological backwardness by simply utilizing imitation strategies in which they are unable to determine and understand cause and effect relationships among technologies and markets, or ②to utilize a strategy of emulation and development of flexible routines aimed at developing sustained competitive advantage through innovation (Li & Kozhikode, 2008). This characterization of emerging economy firms draws attention to their internal resource constraints (Bruton et al. , 2008) and the lack of complementary assets that could enable them to utilize new knowledge effectively (Li & Kozhikode, 2008). Secondly, these are firms that face a range of economic hazards in their home countries. Indeed, their home countries are characterized as undergoing institutional transition (Peng, 2003) as well as exhibiting institutional voids—defined as a paucity of specialized market intermediaries (Ricart et al. , 2004). These are countries that have weak capital market structures, poorly specified property rights, and high environmental uncertainty (Li, 2013).

---

① The dependent variable in the current study is innovative performance and we define this as the ability of the firm to generate new patents, develop new products, and create sales based on new products.

Increasingly, firms from emerging economies have pursued outward foreign direct investment (FDI) in order to achieve both sales growth and strategic learning. The have often been encouraged by their national governments to do this, as well as the openness of many developed markets (Deng, 2009). Foreign market knowledge is therefore important for emerging economy firms seeking to develop innovative capabilities (Li, Chen & Shapiro, 2010). Nevertheless, when such firms are new to internationalization—lacking experience in operating in foreign markets—the link between foreign market knowledge and innovative performance is not always clear cut. Consequently, scholars have called for more research on the links between internationalization and innovative performance of emerging economy firms (Li et al. , 2010; Luo & Tung, 2007; Zhang & Li, 2010).

We address this call in the current study by developing and testing a model that predicts how innovative performance in an emerging economy firm will be directly influenced by the foreign market knowledge it gains through its initial international expansion. We draw on the knowledge – based view of the multinational enterprise (MNE) (Grant, 1996; Kogut & Zander, 1993; Zander, 2002) and organizational learning theory (Fiol & Lyles, 1985; Huber, 1991; March, 1991) to develop our hypotheses. Our model also accounts for a hitherto under – researched indirect moderating effect of country sales breadth, defined as the proclivity of the firm to seek expansion into a variety of new countries in a given period of time. Expressed another way, we assume that foreign market knowledge will be beneficial for innovative performance, should managers of emerging market firms seek to gain this knowledge through a few select countries, or extend their presence in a larger number of countries? To the best of our knowledge, this question has not been addressed in prior research. We present two competing theoretical perspectives on this issue, based, firstly, on the logic of diversity and, secondly, on the logic of time compression diseconomies. Thus we recognize the potential for both benefits and costs in early expansion of firms from an emerging economy. While the former emphasizes the role that diverse experiences play in novelty and creativity that underpin innovation (Dell'Era & Verganti, 2010; Wanous & Youtz, 1986; Zahra et al. , 2000), the latter argues that firms face constraints because of their limited capacity to handle and absorb the complexities that accompany international expansion (Jiang, Beamish & Makino, 2013; Vermeulen & Barkema, 2002; Williams & Lee, 2009), accompanied by high coordination costs during initial expansion (Lu & Beamish, 2004).

Our fieldwork is based on a questionnaire survey of senior managers in 92 Chinese small – to – medium – sized enterprises that have embarked on international expansion. China is an ideal setting to conduct this study. While commentators have noted that the competitive capability of China's firms is relatively weak, China has gone through incredible economic growth in the last several decades (Choi & Williams, 2012; Li et al. , 2010) and its firms have become more innovative. With the erosion in the cost advantage of Chinese manufacturing, Chinese firms need to develop innovative capabilities to be more competitive in the Chinese market and abroad (Gu & Tse, 2010; Hu & Jefferson, 2004). The Chinese government has formulated a *going global* policy to encourage international expansion of Chinese firms in technology sectors (Buckley et al. , 2007; Zhang, Li & Schoonhoven, 2009).

The findings of our study show that foreign market knowledge has a significant and positive impact on innovative performance, and that this relationship is positively moderated by country sales breadth. We also identify subtle but interesting non – linear effects. We contribute to the literature on internationalization and innovative performance in emerging economy firms by showing how knowledge gained through initial expansion in overseas markets is useful for innovative capability development. We also contribute to the debate on diversity and time compression diseconomies by showing how a greater proclivity for expanding into new countries will boost, rather than constrain, innovation for emerging economy firms. This offers support for a theory of innovation in emerging economy firms based on learning from diversity in foreign markets. The results also have implications for managers in emerging market firms relating to the conditions under which international expansion and knowledge acquisition from international markets can be used for innovation.

2. Theory and Model Development

In their seminal work on the internationalization process, Johanson and Vahlne (1977) argued that international expansion is a process of gradual knowledge accumulation. Firms collect knowledge about foreign markets through their increasing commitment and operations in the market. As firms operate abroad they learn about their clients, their needs, resources and limitations. Operations in international markets allow firms to accumulate international knowledge and experience that can be used to respond to opportunities and deal with foreign market uncertainties (Andersen, 1993). This stream of internationalization research draws on organizational learning theory to provide a foundation for explaining the international growth of firms. Experience and foreign market knowledge are seen as key success factors for multinational enterprises (MNEs) undertaking foreign direct investment, with benefits both for performance of foreign subsidiaries as well as the overall corporation (Barkema, Bell & Pennings, 1996; Barkema & Drogendijk, 2007; Barkema, Shenkar, Vermeulen & Bell, 1997).

The knowledge – based view of the MNE regards knowledge as a source of sustainable competitive advantage; knowledge acquired from foreign markets can be utilized to create and augment the competitive capabilities of the firm (Gupta & Govindarajan, 2000; Kogut & Zander, 1993; Kuemmerle, 2002). Scholars in this tradition have suggested that the most important asset for firms is knowledge and the most important capabilities are how to learn and to utilize that learning (Grant, 1996; Petersen, Pedersen & Lyles, 2008; Zander, 2002). According to this view, the "organizational advantage" (Ghoshal & Moran, 1996) of firms over markets arises from their superior capability in creating and transferring knowledge. While it has long been recognized that knowledge acquisition opens new "productive opportunities" (Penrose, 1995) and enhances the firm's ability to exploit these opportunities, it is less understood how this mechanism works for emerging economy firms (Horng & Chen, 2008; Jefferson, Huamao, Xiaojing & Xiaoyun, 2006; Li et al. , 2010). Research suggests that the development and growth of emerging economy firms would be dependent upon combining their own firm specific knowledge with that of external sources to augment home base knowledge or create competence through international expansion (Kuemmerle, 1999; Mathews & Cho, 1999; Meyer & Thaijongrak, 2012). However, emerging economy firms differ from firms in developed economies, which generally leverage and exploit ownership – specific advantages in foreign countries (Dunning, 1998; Lecraw, 1983; Cardoza & Fornes, 2011). The international expansion of firms from emerging economies is often triggered by "pull" factors such as the desire to acquire advanced technology, obtain managerial expertise to overcome their latecomer handicap (Luo & Tung,

2007). It has been noted that emerging markets firms are often superior in combining and integrating outside technologies and knowledge with their own knowledge base (Luo, Sun & Wang, 2011).

2.1 Baseline Hypothesis: Foreign Market Knowledge and Innovative Performance

Despite the fact that various approaches have been proposed to identify the drivers of innovation, there is no over – riding theory of innovation (Choi & Williams, 2012). Organizational learning theorists (Barkema & Vermeulen, 1998; Lyles & Salk, 1996; Zahra & Garvis, 2000; Zahra et al. , 2000) suggest that international expansion can enhance the learning of new skills and capabilities that significantly improve a firm's ability to innovate, take risks and develop new revenue streams. Innovations arise as a consequence of new combinations of knowledge and other resources accumulated over time (Cohen & Levinthal, 1990; Kogut & Zander, 1992, 1993; Schumpeter & Opie, 1955). As emphasized in the internationalization process theory (Yli – Renko, Autio & Tontti, 2002), foreign market knowledge is the acquisition of information and experiential knowledge concerning foreign markets, competitors, customers, and potential cooperation partners. Scholars have noted that acquisition of foreign market knowledge gained through international expansion can facilitate innovation within the firm (Barkema & Vermeulen, 1998; Cantwell & Piscitello, 2000; Kuemmerle, 1999; Zahra, Ireland & Hitt, 2000; Zanfei, 2000). Firms competing in international markets can draw from multiple knowledge bases in their research and development, manufacturing, and marketing operations to learn new skills that augment current capabilities (Zahra et al. , 2000). Thus, success of international firms early in their evolution can be achieved by leveraging innovativeness, knowledge and capabilities (Knight & Cavusgil, 2004). Highlighted as an approach of learning and competence creation, international expansion has been suggested to provide fertile ground for firms to acquire knowledge and increase their innovative performance (Cantwell & Mudambi, 2005; Kuemmerle, 1999; Tsao & Chen, 2012; Zanfei, 2000). Presutti et al. (2007) found that foreign market knowledge can enhance the breadth of firms' knowledge available to increase the potential for new sources and ideas concerning innovative task performance as well as increase the willingness of firms to develop new R&D activity, which is usually considered as a way to generate and integrate internal knowledge source for innovation (Atuahene − Gima & Ko, 2001; Li et al. , 2010; Zhou & Li, 2008).

Multinational firms from developed economies can generate the requisite knowledge for innovation internally through in − house research and development (R&D) and marketing and externally through channels such as strategic alliances and acquisitions (Ahuja & Katila, 2001; Chandy, Hopstaken, Narasimhan & Prabhu, 2006; Li et al. , 2010; Zhou & Li, 2008). Emerging economy firms, as latecomers, typically face disadvantages that limit innovation. They do not have the internal knowledge or capabilities to engage in extensive R&D activities, and thus access to external, advanced foreign knowledge is crucial for firms in emerging economies to improve their innovative capabilities. To overcome these disadvantages, firms in emerging markets require access to superior foreign technology and customer knowledge, essential for fostering product innovation (Li & Atuahene − Gima, 2001). In line with the arguments above, we propose that the more foreign market knowledge which emerging economy firms gain through international expansion, the more likely they are able to develop and deploy their innovative capability. Therefore, we hypothesize:

H1: *Foreign market knowledge has a positive impact on the innovative performance of firms from an emerging economy.*

2. 2   Competing Views on the Moderating Effect of Country Sales Breadth

One of the key issues confronting firms in an emerging economy that seek to enhance their innovative performance through foreign market knowledge is how many countries to attempt to generate sales from while accessing and capturing new market knowledge. Country sales breadth relates to diversity in the countries in which the firm derives its sales. At one extreme, newly internationalizing firms may generate sales within one or two foreign markets. At another extreme, they may disperse their business operations across a large variety of foreign markets. Scholars have noted how these alternatives will yield different learning outcomes (Hashai, 2011; Vermeulen & Barkema, 2002). On the one hand, an emphasis on a large number of countries will generate diversity in experiences which may be beneficial for innovation. Diversity is recognized as a source of creativity and innovation that can provide a basis for competitive advantage (Barkema & Vermeulen, 1998). On the other hand, firms may encounter diseconomies of time compression (Vermeulen & Barkema, 2002), drawing erroneous inferences because they are not able to effectively coordinate an abundance of new knowledge from foreign markets. They will learn incorrectly from their early expansions when facing dissimilar circumstances, knowledge may be discerned as irrelevant and inappropriate (Zeng et al. , 2013).

These potential advantages and disadvantages associated with country sales breadth puts the internationalizing emerging economy firms in a paradoxical situation (Bassett – Jones, 2005). At both extremes of country sales breadth, the firm is able to access foreign market knowledge ($H1$ above). But to what extent will country sales breadth moderate the relationship between foreign market knowledge and innovative performance? We present two competing perspectives on this based on the logic of diversity and on the logic of time compression diseconomies and knowledge coordination.

Firstly, in order to innovate, a firm must first search, identify and evaluate knowledge from different sources. International expansion exposes the firm to new environments that have different systems of organization, inducing firms to understand best practices in foreign markets (Dess et al. , 2003). The diversity of foreign cultures, consumer groups, and political systems associated with international expansion broaden the firm's search for new knowledge (March, 1991). Operating in diverse circumstances increases the variety of events and ideas to which a firm is exposed (Huber, 1991), leading to a more extensive knowledge base (Barkema & Vermeulen, 1998). In addition, given that countries differ in their systems of innovation (Nelson, 1993), firms that venture across a large number of international borders could benefit from their exposure to these different innovation systems, enabling them to conceive new ideas, systems, processes, and products (Henderson & Cockburn, 1994). Previous empirical investigations have generally provided support for the argument that diversity in an organization's knowledge base is a source of innovation that can provide a basis for competitive advantage (Bassett – Jones, 2005; Dell'Era & Verganti, 2010; Wanous & Youtz, 1986). Zahra et al. (2000) suggested that knowledge diversity increases the depth, breadth, and speed of learning, leading to a greater number of product introductions. Fiol (1994) argued that diversity is important for collective learning and corporate innovation, as long as there is a shared way of framing differences within corporate communications. CEOs of internationally diversified firms have richer knowledge structures than CEOs of domestic firms (Calori, Johnson & Sarnin, 1994). The greater diversity in the knowledge of managers and other workers aggregates to richer knowledge structures at the level of the firm (Walsh, 1995), and stronger technological capabilities (Cohen & Levinthal, 1990). Grant (1987) suggested that the degree of internationalization itself should confer advantage for MNEs, giving them opportunities to exploit intangible resources, use market power, spread their market risks, and to seek less expensive inputs and less price – sensitive markets (Kim, Hwang & Burgers, 1993). Internationally diverse firms have access to the resources necessary to build innovation capabilities. For example, they are exposed to new and diverse ideas from multiple market and cultural perspectives (Hitt, Hoskisson & Kim, 1997). The diversity of a firm's international business environment enhances its knowledge stocks through learning based on interactions with local knowledge bases. Scholars have shown how the range of countries increases the speed of knowledge processing and reduces product development cycles (Zahra et al., 2000). Hence:

H2a: Country sales breadth positively moderates the relationship between foreign market knowledge and innovative performance of firms in an emerging economy.

An alternative view is that seeking country sales breadth by venturing into many different countries is a complicated process compared to concentrating on a limited number of geographic markets. The notion that prior experience may benefit subsequent activities by generating valuable knowledge is based on the premise that firms can effectively untangle causalities in prior activities and draw accurate inferences (Levinthal & March, 1993). Organizational learning theorists have acknowledged that this premise is often violated by factors such as ambiguity and paucity of experience, as well as by the rational and cognitive limitations of individuals (Fiol & Lyles, 1985; Huber, 1991; Levinthal & March, 1993; Levitt & March, 1988; Zeng et al., 2013). One firm's ability to learn from another firm depends on the similarity of firms' ①knowledge bases, ②organizational structures and compensation policies, and ③dominant logics (Lane & Lubatkin, 1998).

Furthermore, the literature on diversity's positive role in innovation tends to ignore the cost associated with the acquisition, assimilation, and transformation of new knowledge (Wales, Parida & Patel, 2013). More internationalized firms will encounter higher volumes of knowledge and will suffer more from the resource – consuming cost implications of coordinating knowledge (Eriksson, Johanson, Majkgard & Sharma, 1997; Lu & Beamish, 2004) than less internationalized firms. Escalating geographic dispersion can greatly increase managerial information – processing demands (Hitt, Hoskisson & Ireland, 1994; Jones & Hill, 1988). Geographic dispersion increases coordination, distribution, and management costs. Firms have to learn how to operate in a variety of institutional and cultural settings and thus adapt their systems, processes, and organizational structures to the international setting. As a result, an increase in country sales breadth will lead to diminished returns in firms' innovative performance.

Drawing from the notion of absorptive capacity, Vermeumen and Barkema (2002) proposed that the larger the geographic scope of an expansion process, the more time the firm needs to fully absorb the accompanying experiences. Firms expanding into many geographical markets suffer more from time compression diseconomies than firms that just disperse into several markets. The more countries involved in an expansion strategy, the more difficult it becomes to absorb the experience, leading to diseconomies of time compression. Hence:

H2b: Country sales breadth negatively moderates the relationship between foreign market knowledge and innovative performance of firms in an emerging economy.

2. 3   Curvilinear Effects

We now combine the logic of diversity and time compression in the emerging economy firm context to argue that the relationship between foreign market knowledge and innovative performance of emerging economy firms will be non – linear. Firstly, the coordination cost problems that are associated with internationalization (Eriksson et al. , 1997; Lu & Beamish, 2004) and that result in knowledge coordination being a challenge for the internationalizing firm are more likely to have a greater impact for emerging economy firms at lower levels of foreign market knowledge. Such firms will suffer from relative technological backwardness (Li, 2013) and lower levels of complementary knowledge assets in their home country that limit their ability to make sense of newly acquired knowledge from foreign sales. Institutional voids in the home country will also mean a paucity of experience for the firm to draw on that will enable the emerging economy firm to overcome issues arising out of a lack of knowledge – relatedness. Secondly, as levels of foreign market knowledge increase, it becomes increasingly likely that international knowledge sources are more diverse. We argued above (*H2a*) that international diversity will expose the firm to wider range of ideas and sources of inspiration for conceiving new products. Building on this, we argue that the problems facing the emerging economy firm in terms of lower levels of complementary assets and presence of institutional voids will gradually be overcome as foreign market knowledge increases and becomes more diverse. Thus there will be limited impact of diversity in foreign market knowledge at lower levels, but at higher levels, diversity will be more likely to stimulate innovative performance by enabling the emerging economy firm to make more sense of foreign market knowledge such that they are more effective in determining how resources are allocated to innovation. Hence:

H3: There is a U – shaped relationship between foreign market knowledge and innovative performance of firms in an emerging economy.

3. Methodology

3.1　Sample and Data Collection

We tested these hypotheses using a questionnaire survey of senior managers who were in charge of international businesses for their respective firms. We used China as our empirical context. This was an ideal setting as the Chinese government has instigated *"going global"* ("zou chu qu") initiative aiming to encourage its firms to internationalize to promote the international competitiveness of Chinese firms (Buckley et al. , 2007). Due to difficulty in collecting primary data from firms in China (Brouthers & Xu, 2002; Peng & Luo, 2000), we identified respondents through both formal and informal networks. We conducted a pre – test and pilot study ahead of the full data collection, and adopted a convenience sampling approach in each stage. For the pre – test and pilot study we conducted interviews with 20 managers of internationalizing Chinese firms based on Shanghai, and issued a draft version of the questionnaire to these managers. Based on the feedback we received, the measures were refined to ensure their relevance to the Chinese context.

A portion of the sample was collected with the help of Suzhou Chamber of Commerce and some of respondents were also identified through informal

networks. The questionnaires were also distributed in China Small & Medi
um – Sized Enterprises (SMEs) Forum supported by Chinese Ministry of
Commerce. The forum, held in Shanghai in September 2007, provided a
platform for communication and interaction between government officials,
business leaders and entrepreneurs in SMEs as well as promoting cooperation
and development during the internationalization process of SMEs. The theme
of this forum is innovation in internationalization paths and patterns of Chi
nese SMEs. At the conference, the survey was conducted through face – to –
face interviews with delegates. This procedure allowed us to assess the suita
bility of the respondents for the study. It also offered respondents an opportu
nity to ask for clarifications about the variables under study. A cover letter in
Chinese was used to explain the purpose of the survey and all of the respond
ents were informed of the voluntary nature of the survey and confidentiality of
their responses. Each respondent was given a small gift as a token of our ap
preciation.

The questionnaire instrument was developed initially in English, using
standard scales. We translated the questionnaire items from English to Chi
nese prior to data collection. From 387 questionnaires issued, we received
168 completed questionnaires. We removed those from the analysis that had
not undertaken foreign direct investment (i. e., merely engaged in expor
ting) and those firms with very low degree of internationalization (the ratio of
foreign sales to total sales less than 5%) (Zahra et al., 2000). After elimi
nating observations with missing values, the sample size was 92 firms (an ef
fective response rate of 23. 8%). The characteristics of the sample are shown
in Table 1. The sample was mixed in terms of industry (traditional manufac
turing, information technology and services) and contained relatively young
companies, with an average age of 8. 54 years.

Table 1   Profile of Firms in the Sample

Variable	Distribution (%)
Industry	
—Traditional manufacturing	21. 7
—Information technology	59. 8
—Service	9. 8

续表

Variable	Distribution (%)
—Medical	1. 1
—Intermediary	1. 1
—Other	6. 5
Internationalization	
—within 2 years after start – up	46. 7
—within 2 ~ 3 years after start – up	23. 9
—within 4 ~ 5 years after start – up	12. 0
—within 5 ~ 6 years after start – up	8. 7
—more than 6 years after start – up	8. 7
Number of countries where firm has sales	
—1 ~ 3 countries	51. 1
—4 ~ 6 countries	17. 4
—7 ~ 9 countries	8. 7
—9 ~ 11 countries	8. 7
—More than 11 countries	14. 1
Internationalization stage	
—Domestic marketing	7. 6
—Pre – export stage	2. 2
—Experimental involvement	32. 6
—Active involvement	26. 1
—Committed involvement	31. 5

3. 2　Measurements

For all scales, Cronbach's α was above the minimum recommended level (Nunnally, 1978). We assessed the structure of each scale using a principal component factor analysis. Items loaded on their respective scales correctly and there were no high cross – loadings which would make item to construct associations ambiguous.

Innovative performance: We followed prior research (Ahuja & Katila, 2001; Hagedoorn & Cloodt, 2003; Yli – Renko, Autio & Sapienza, 2001) by operationalizing innovative performance as the speed of new product development, number of annual new products, success rate of product innovation, and sales of new products to total sales. Cronbach's α for this scale was

0. 87. We ran additional tests with the dependent variable as annual patents, i. e. , capturing innovation performance prior to commercialization.

Foreign market knowledge: Foreign market knowledge was operationalized using a four – item scale capturing the top managers' knowledge about their foreign competitors, the needs of foreign clients/customers, foreign distribution channels, and effective marketing in foreign markets. This scale is adapted from an established scale in prior literature (Yli – Renko et al. , 2002; Zhou, 2007). Cronbach's α for this scale was 0. 86.

Country sales breadth: Two indicators were used to measure this: the number of countries entered (Fernhaber, Gilbert & McDougall, 2008; Zahra et al. , 2000) as well as the degree to which foreign sales contributed to total sales. Cronbach's α for this scale was 0. 64.

We conducted a confirmatory factor analysis (CFA) to assess construct validity. The measurement model provides a satisfactory fit to the data (Goodness – of – fit index [CFI] = 0. 97, Incremental fit index [IFI] = 0. 97, root mean square error of approximation [RMSEA] = 0. 06). Moreover, all factor loadings are highly significant ($p < 0.001$), and the composite reliabilities (CR) of all construct exceed the 0. 70 benchmark (Fornell & Larcker, 1981). All average variances extracted (AVE) except one are greater than 0. 50. Thus the measures demonstrate adequate convergent validity and reliability (Fornell & Larcker, 1981). We also calculated the maximum shared variance (MSV) between all possible pairs of constructs to determine whether they are lower than the AVE of the individual constructs. For each construct, the AVE is higher than MSV with the other constructs. The results indicate that our measures possess adequate reliability and validity (Table 2).

Table 2   Measurement Items and Validity Assessment

Variables and Questionnaire Item (5 point scales)	Loadings
Innovative performance(Cronbach's α = 0. 88, CR = 0. 88, AVE = 0. 60, MSV = 0. 17)	
Speed of new product development	0. 85
Number of annual new products	0. 84
Success rate of product innovation	0. 76
Sales of new products to total sales	0. 78
Number of annual patents	0. 74

续表

Variables and Questionnaire Item (5 point scales)	Loadings
Foreign market knowledge（Cronbach's α = 0.86, CR = 0.86, AVE = 0.60, MSV = 0.29）	
Top managers' knowledge about…	
…foreign competitors	0.74
…the needs of foreign clients / customers	0.83
…foreign distribution channels	0.79
…effective marketing in foreign markets	0.75
Country sales breadth（Cronbach's α = 0.64, CR = 0.66, AVE = 0.50, MSV = 0.29）	
Number of overseas markets in which firm has sales	0.82
% foreign sales / total sales	0.58

Factor analysis also allows us to test for common method bias. A model with a single factor linking all 12 items from the dependent and independent variables was assessed. This model did not fit the data. Moreover, we conducted a rotated component analysis on these 12 items. We obtained three components, corresponding to our three constructs. We do not believe common method bias is likely to impact our interpretation of the results.

We also included controls for several variables that might affect the hypothesized relationships. We included firm age as a control variable, as this may have an influence on knowledge exploitation through experience effects (Autio, Sapienza & Almeida, 2000; Zahra et al. , 2000). Firm age was measured by the number of years the company had been in existence. We controlled for firm size, common in analysis of innovative performance (Cohen & Levinthal, 1989), measured by the natural logarithm of a firm full time employees. As industries vary in knowledge acquisition (Yli – Renko et al. , 2001), we controlled for industry (self – reported as the primary industry from which the company generated most of its sales). Following Autio (2000), we also controlled for the firm's speed of internationalization. This was captured as the time in years between a firm's founding and its first international sales. We also controlled for location because location can influence innovative performance through local knowledge acquisition (Christensen & Drejer, 2005). The locations were Shanghai, Jiangsu, Zhejiang, Guangdong, Beijing, Shangdong, Anhui, Liaoning and Tianjin.

4. Results

Table 3 presents the means, standard deviations, and inter – correlations for all variables used in the study. All variables were normally distributed. As anticipated the correlation between firm age and size is positive and significant (r = 0. 59, p < 0. 01). Also, as one would expect, the older and larger firms in the sample were at a later stage of internationalization (r = 0. 24, p < 0. 05; r = 0. 28, p < 0. 01). We note that there is a positive and significant bi – variate correlation between innovative performance and foreign market knowledge (r = 0. 47, p < 0. 01) and between innovative performance and country sales breadth (r = 0. 29, p < 0. 01). The firms that emphasized greater country sales breadth were also larger, older, and at a later stage of internationalization. In the latter case, the correlation was large (r = 0. 54, p < 0. 01). Nevertheless, we examined the variance inflation factor and tolerance values for all independent variables and found that the effect of the correlated independent variables would not hamper the interpretability of the results.

Table 3   Means, Standard Deviations, and Correlations

Variables	Mean	S. D.	1	2	3	4	5	6
1. Innovative performance [a]	3. 44	0. 79						
2. Annual patents [b]	3. 10	1. 01	0. 64 ***					
3. Size (ln)	5. 20	1. 60	0. 05	0. 16				
4. Age	8. 54	5. 11	0. 04	0. 17	0. 59 ***			
5. Industry	3. 72	1. 16	− 0. 12	− 0. 10	− 0. 15	− 0. 09		
6. Intern. speed	2. 74	1. 47	0. 07	0. 34 ***	0. 13	0. 19 +	− 0. 11	
7. Location	2. 18	1. 96	0. 25 *	0. 14	0. 28 **	0. 20 +	− 0. 15	0. 00
8. Foreign market knowledge	3. 37	0. 78	0. 46 **	0. 37 **	0. 21 *	− 0. 04	0. 06	0. 14
9. Country sales breadth	2. 46	1. 27	0. 24 *	0. 35 ***	0. 25 *	− 0. 12	0. 13	0. 11

Note: N = 92 *** p < 0. 001, ** p < 0. 01, * p < 0. 05, + p < 0. 1.

a Based on four item scale for new product development and launch success.

b Single item.

The results of the multiple regression analysis are shown in Tables 4, 5 and 6. Four separate models were used to test the effects of control variables, direct effects, moderating effects and non – linear effects. In each analysis, with the full model, we note the highest variance explained by the full model with non – linear effects. In all models, foreign market knowledge is positive and significant, providing strong support for *H1* （p < 0.001）. We also note a positive and significant moderating effect of country sales breadth on the relationship between foreign market knowledge and innovative performance in the moderating effects models. This provides support for *H2 a* and not for *H2 b*. The interaction plot showing support for *H2 a* is presented in Figure 1. The curvilinear models have significant coefficients for the entered term and the quadratic term for foreign market knowledge. This provides support for *H3* , which argues that there is a U – shaped relationship between foreign market knowledge and innovative performance in emerging economy firms. The plot for this is shown in Figure 2. As an exploratory extension we examine the profile of coefficients for the model with satisfaction with annual patents as a single item dependent variable. Results are tabulated in Table 6. Here we note that internationalization speed （a categorical variable capturing the time to first internationalization investment） has a positive and significant impact on satisfaction with patents. This indicates that respondents were more satisfied with patent performance the earlier the firm's initial foreign expansion. We also note a significant and negative interaction between country sales breadth and the quadratic term for foreign market knowledge. The plot for this result is shown in Figure 3. This rather unexpected finding shows how an increase in country sales breadth may lead to dissatisfaction with patent performance and how this becomes more acute as foreign market knowledge increases.

Table 4　Regression Results （1）

		Innovative Performance （5 item scale）			
		1	2	3	4
Controls	Size	− 0.01	0.002	− 0.01	0.01
		(0.06)	(0.06)	(0.06)	(0.06)
	Age	− 0.00	− 0.01	− 0.01	− 0.01
		(0.02)	(0.18)	(0.02)	(0.02)

续表

Innovative Performance (5 item scale)					
		1	2	3	4
Controls	Industry	−0.03 (0.05)	−0.03 (0.04)	−0.03 (0.04)	−0.03 (0.04)
	Location	0.09* (0.04)	0.07+ (0.04)	0.07+ (0.04)	0.06 (0.04)
	Intern. Speed	0.08 (0.06)	0.08 (0.06)	0.10+ (0.06)	0.10+ (0.06)
Independent variables	FMK		**0.38*** (0.08)**	**0.41*** (0.08)**	**0.42*** (0.08)**
	CSB		−0.06 (0.08)	−0.10 (0.09)	−0.05 (0.10)
	FMK × CSB			**0.15+ (0.08)**	0.06 (0.10)
	FMK^2				**0.12+ (0.07)**
	FMK^2 × CSB				−0.03 (0.07)
	Max. VIF	1.61	1.73	1.76	3.26
	F	1.60	4.81***	4.73***	4.46***
	F Change		11.83***	3.27+	2.55+
	Adj. R^2	0.03	0.23	0.25	0.27

Note: *** $p < 0.001$, ** $p < 0.01$, * $p < 0.05$, + $p < 0.1$ standard errors in parentheses.

Table 5   Regression Results (2)

Innovative Performance (4 item scale)					
		1	2	3	4
Controls	Size	−0.01 (0.07)	−0.003 (0.06)	−0.02 (0.06)	0.01 (0.06)
	Age	−0.002 (0.02)	−0.02 (0.02)	−0.01 (0.02)	−0.01 (0.02)
	Industry	−0.04 (0.05)	−0.04 (0.04)	−0.04 (0.04)	−0.03 (0.04)
	Location	0.10 (0.04)	0.08* (0.04)	0.08* (0.04)	0.07+ (0.04)
	Intern. Speed	0.04 (0.06)	0.04 (0.06)	0.06 (0.06)	0.06 (0.06)

续表

		Innovative Performance (4 item scale)			
		1	2	3	4
Independent variables	FMK		0.39 *** (0.08)	0.42 *** (0.08)	0.40 *** (0.10)
	CSB		-0.09 (0.09)	-0.13 (0.09)	-0.10 (0.10)
	FMK × CSB			0.14 + (0.08)	0.03 (0.1)
	FMK^2				0.13 + (0.07)
	FMK^2 × CSB				0.004 (0.07)
	Max. VIF	1.61	1.73	1.76	3.26
	F	1.41	4.64 ***	4.50 ***	4.19 ***
	F Change		11.86 ***	2.80 +	2.36 +
	Adj. R^2	0.02	0.22	0.24	0.26

Note: *** $p < 0.001$, *** $p < 0.01$, * $p < 0.05$, + $p < 0.1$ standard errors in parentheses.

Table 6 Regression Results (3)

		Satisfaction with Annual Patents			
		1	2	3	4
Controls	Size	0.04 (0.08)	0.02 (0.08)	0.003 (0.08)	0.04 (0.08)
	Age	0.01 (0.02)	-0.002 (0.02)	0.001 (0.02)	-0.01 (0.02)
	Industry	-0.02 (0.06)	-0.02 (0.06)	-0.01 (0.06)	-0.01 (0.06)
	Location	0.06 (0.05)	0.04 (0.05)	0.04 (0.05)	0.01 (0.05)
	Intern. Speed	0.25 ** (0.08)	0.24 ** (0.07)	0.26 *** (0.08)	0.26 *** (0.07)
Independent variables	FMK		0.32 ** (0.11)	0.37 *** (0.11)	0.50 *** (0.13)
	CSB		0.05 (0.11)	-0.004 (0.11)	0.13 (0.13)
	FMK × CSB			0.18 + (0.11)	0.18 (0.13)

续表

		Satisfaction with Annual Patents			
		1	2	3	4
Independent variables	FMK^2				0. 04
					(0. 09)
	FMK^2 × CSB				**− 0. 17 $^+$**
					(0. 10)
	Max. VIF	1. 61	1. 73	1. 76	3. 26
	F	2. 94 *	4. 09 ***	3. 99 ***	3. 93 ***
	F Change		6. 09 **	2. 69 $^+$	2. 94 $^+$
	Adj. R^2	0. 10	0. 19	0. 21	0. 24

Note: *** $p < 0.001$, ** $p < 0.01$, * $p < 0.05$, + $p < 0.1$ Standard errors in parentheses.

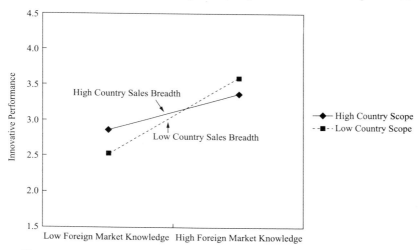

Figure 1　Moderating Effect of Country Sales Breadth on the Relationship between Foreign Market Knowledge and Innovative Peformance

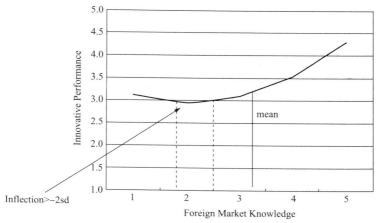

Figure 2　U – Shaped Relationship between Foreign Market Knowledge and Innovative Peformance

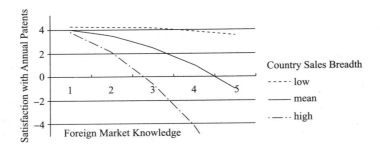

Figure 3　Non–linear Interaction between Country Sales Breadth and Foreign Market Knowledge on Perceptions of Satisfaction with Patent Performance

5. Discussion

Our study contributes to the literature on internationalization and innovative performance in emerging economy firms by showing how knowledge gained through initial sales expansion in overseas markets is useful for innovative capability in these types of firms. This reinforces conventional IB theory on the benefits of internationalization, not only for sales and financial performance, but also for capabilities in the firm that are aimed at technological innovation and new product development. We show that the notion that foreign market knowledge is beneficial for innovative performance is not unique to firms from developed countries. Our findings address calls to examine this question in the context of emerging economies (Li, Chen & Shapiro, 2010) and show that these types of firms—despite the constraints put on them as a result of historical institutional weaknesses—are also able to use foreign market knowledge through sales to boost their innovate performance.

We also contribute to the debate on whether theories of diversity or time compression diseconomies and coordination costs are more powerful in explaining innovative performance. At least in the Chinese setting, the positive influence of diversity through country sales breadth appears to outweigh any costs associated with time compression and knowledge coordination. Our results go some way to showing how emerging economy firms are able to become more innovative through access to foreign market knowledge, despite not having the long multi–decade experience of operating in many international markets in the same way that developed economy firms have. The findings suggest that such firms are able to access and integrate knowledge from diverse sources and that this capability has a positive influence on how foreign market knowledge drives innovation. This offers support for a theory of innovation in emerging economy firms based on learning from diversity in foreign markets. We show how a greater proclivity for expanding sales into new countries appears to boost, rather than constrain, innovation. The results also have implications for managers in emerging economy firms relating to the conditions under which international expansion and knowledge acquisition from international markets can be used for innovation. One implication is that firms should be aware of the acquisition of foreign market knowledge in their internationalization process and view it as vital for improving their innovative capabilities. They should actively engage in such activities to speed up knowledge acquisition and capability building. Also, firms in emerging economies should pay attention to location choice for their foreign expansion and establish subsidiaries in the locations where they can tap into the available pools of knowledge. These results also show the critical importance of the ability to manage country sales breadth when firms seek expansion into a variety of new countries. Although diversity confer learning advantages over domestic firms, effective implementation and management of diversity are necessary to realize the benefit.

There are a number of limitations to the current study that can be addressed in future work. Firstly, the sample size is rather small, and although we collected 168 returns, 76 of these were not usable due to our requirement to examine only those firms that had control over foreign assets and that had the degree of internationalization (measured as the ratio of foreign sales to total sales) above 5%. It is difficult to generalize from this final sample size and future research can continue this investigation by considering firms from other industries and locations in China. Secondly, we focused on Chinese firms. It is possible that firm internationalization and innovative capability development in other emerging economies follows a different development trajectory due to different institutional pressures (Lamin & Livanis, 2013). While China is a suitable setting to conduct this type of study, future work can compare China with the internationalization and innovation outcomes of firms in other emerging economies, such as ones that are still at an early of beginner stage of institutional transition (Li, 2013). Thirdly, we did not examine the structures and processes within the firm that enables it to access and integrate knowledge (Zander, 2002). While we show support for the argument that diversity through country sales breadth will have a positive impact on the relationship between foreign market knowledge and innovative performance, we do not show how the firms in our sample were able to acquire and integrate this knowledge such that innovative capabilities in the home country could be bolstered. Future research could investigate these internal mechanisms to ascertain whether Chinese firms tend to use specific integrative mechanisms that are idiosyncratic to Chinese management or to emerging economy firms. We hope that these steps will help build our understanding of how firms in emerging economies can leverage internationalization in order to become more innovative.

References

Ahuja, G. & Katila, R. 2001. Technological acquisitions and the innovation performance of acquiring firms: A longitudinal study. *Strategic Management Journal*, 22(3): 197 – 220.

Andersen, O. 1993. On the internationalization process of firms—A critical analysis. *Journal of International Business Studies*, 24(2): 209 – 231.

Atuahene – Gima, K. & Ko, A. 2001. An empirical investigation of the effect of market orientation and entrepreneurship orientation alignment on product innovation. *Organization Science*, 12(1): 54 – 74.

Autio, E., Sapienza, H. J. & Almeida, J. G. 2000. Effects of age at entry, knowledge intensity, and imitability on international growth. *Academy of Management Journal*, 43(5): 909 – 924.

Barkema, H. G., Bell, J. H. J. & Pennings, J. M. 1996. Foreign entry, cultural barriers, and learning. *Strategic Management Journal*, 17(2): 151 – 166.

Barkema, H. G. & Drogendijk, R. 2007. Internationalising in small, incremental or larger steps? *Journal of International Business Studies*, 38(7): 1132 – 1148.

Barkema, H. G. Shenkar, O., Vermeulen, F., & Bell, J. H. J. 1997. Working abroad, working with others: How firms learn to operate international joint ventures. *Academy of Management Journal*, 40(2): 426 – 442.

Barkema, H. G. & Vermeulen, F. 1998. International expansion through start – up or acquisition: A learning perspective. *Academy of Management Journal*, 41(1): 7 – 26.

Bassett – Jones, N. 2005. The paradox of diversity management, creativity and innovation. *Creativity and Innovation Management*, 14(2): 169 – 175.

Brouthers, L. E. & Xu, K. F. 2002. Product stereotypes, strategy and performance satisfaction: The case of Chinese exporters. *Journal of International Business Studies*,

33(4): 657 – 677.

Bruton, G. D. Ahlstrom, D. , & Obloj, K. (2008). Entrepreneurship in emerging economies: Where are we today and where should the research go in the future. *Entrepreneurship Theory and Practice*, 32(1), 1 – 14.

Buckley, P. J. Clegg, L. J. , Cross, A. R. , Liu, X. , Voss, H. , & Zheng, P. 2007.
The determinants of Chinese outward foreign direct investment. *Journal of International Business Studies*, 38(4): 499 – 518.

Calori, R. Johnson, G. , & Sarnin, P. 1994. CEO's cognitive maps and the scope of the
organization. *Strategic Management Journal*, 15(6): 437 – 457.

Cantwell, J. & Mudambi, R. 2005. MNE competence – creating subsidiary mandates.
Strategic Management Journal, 26(12): 1109 – 1128.

Cantwell, J. & Piscitello, L. 2000. Accumulating technological competence: Its changing
impact on corporate diversification and internationalization. *Industrial and Corporate
Change*, 9(1): 21 – 51.

Cardoza, G. & Fornes, G. 2011. The internationalisation of SMEs from China: The case
of Ningxia Hui Autonomous Region. *Asia Pacific Journal of Management*, 28(4):
737 – 759.

Chandy, R. Hopstaken, B. , Narasimhan, O. , & Prabhu, J. 2006. From invention to
innovation: Conversion ability in product development. *Journal of Marketing Research*,43(3): 494 – 508.

Choi, S. B. & Williams, C. 2012. The impact of innovation intensity, scope, and spillovers on sales growth in Chinese firms. *Asia Pacific Journal of Management*. doi:
10. 1007/s10490 – 012 – 9329 – 1.

Christensen, J. & Drejer, I. 2005. The strategic importance of location: Location decisions and the effects of firm location on innovation and knowledge acquisition. *European Planning Studies*, 13(6): 807 – 814.

Cohen, W. M. & Levinthal, D. A. 1989. Innovation and Learning—The 2 faces of R
and D. *Economic Journal*, 99(397): 569 – 596.

Cohen, W. M. & Levinthal, D. A. 1990. Absorptive capacity—A new perspective on
learning and innovation. *Administrative Science Quarterly*, 35(1): 128 – 152.

DellEra, C. & Verganti, R. 2010. Collaborative strategies in design – intensive industries: Knowledge diversity and innovation. *Long Range Planning*, 43 (1):
123 – 141.

Deng, P. 2009. Why do Chinese firms tend to acquire strategic assets in international expansion? *Journal of World Business*, 44(1): 74 – 84.

Dess, G. G. Ireland, R. D. , Zahra, S. A. , Floyd, S. W. , Janney, J. J. , & Lane,
P. J. 2003. Emerging issues in corporate entrepreneurship. *Journal of Management*, 29(3): 351 – 378.

Dunning, J. H. 1998. Location and the multinational enterprise: A neglected factor?

Journal of International Business Studies, 29(1): 45 – 66.

Eriksson, K. Johanson, J. , Majkgard, A. & Sharma, D. D. 1997. Experiential knowl-edge and cost in the internationalization process. *Journal of International Business Studies*, 28(2): 337 – 360.

Fernhaber, S. A. Gilbert, B. A. , & McDougall, P. P. 2008. International entrepre-neurship and geographic location: An empirical examination of new venture interna-tionalization. *Journal of International Business Studies*, 39(2): 267 – 290.

Fiol, C. M. & Lyles, M. A. 1985. Organizational learning. *Academy of Management Re-view*, 10(4): 803 – 813.

Fornell, C. & Larcker, D. F. 1981. Evaluating structural equation models with unobserv-able variables and measurement error. *Journal of Marketing Research*, 18(1): 39 – 50.

Gaur, A. S. & Lu, J. W. 2007. Ownership strategies and survival of foreign subsidiar-ies: Impacts of institutional distance and experience. *Journal of Management*, 33 (1): 84 – 110.

Ghoshal, S. & Moran, P. 1996. Bad for practice: A critique of the transaction cost theo-ry. *Academy of Management Review*, 21(1) : 13 – 47.

Grant, R. M. 1996. Toward a knowledge – based theory of the firm. *Strategic Manage-ment Journal*, 17(SI): 109 – 122.

Gu, M. & Tse, E. 2010. Building innovative organizations in China: The "execution + " organization. *Asia Pacific Journal of Management*, 27(1): 25 – 53.

Guan, J. C. Mok, C. K. , Yam, R. , Chin, K. & Pun, K. F. 2006. Technology trans-fer and innovation performance: Evidence from Chinese firms. *Technological Fore-casting and Social Change*, 73(6): 666 – 678.

Gupta, A. K. & Govindarajan, V. 2000. Knowledge flows within multinational corpora-tions. *Strategic Management Journal*, 21(4): 473 – 496.

Hagedoorn, J. & Cloodt, M. 2003. Measuring innovative performance: Is there an advan-tage in using multiple indicators? *Research Policy*, 32(8): 1365 – 1379.

Hashai, N. 2011. Sequencing the expansion of geographic scope and foreign operations by "born global" firms. *Journal of International Business Studies*, 42(8): 995 – 1015.

Henderson, R. & Cockburn, I. 1994. Measuring competence? Exploring firm effects in pharmaceutical research. *Strategic Management Journal*, 15(S1): 63 – 84.

Hitt, M. A. , Hoskisson, R. E. & Ireland, R. D. 1994. A mid – range theory of the in-teractive effects of international and product diversification on innovation and per-formance. *Journal of Management*, 20(2): 297 – 326.

Hitt, M. A. , Hoskisson, R. E. & Kim, H. 1997. International diversification: Effects on innovation and firm performance in product – diversified firms. *Academy of Man-agement Journal*, 40(4): 767 – 798.

Horng, C. & Chen, W. 2008. From contract manufacturing to own brand management:

The role of learning and cultural heritage identity. *Management and Organization Review*, 4(1): 109 – 133.

Hu, A. G. & Jefferson, G. H. 2004. Returns to research and development in Chinese industry: Evidence from state – owned enterprises in Beijing. *China Economic Review*, 15(1): 86 – 107.

Huber, G. P. 1991. Organizational learning: The contributing processes and the literatures. *Organization Science*, 2(1): 88 – 115.

Jefferson, G. H. Huamao, B. , Xiaojing, G. , & Xiaoyun, Y. 2006. R&D performance in Chinese industry. *Economics of Innovation and New Technology*, 15 (4 – 5): 345 – 366.

Jiang, R. J. Beamish, P. W. & Makino, S. 2013. Time compression diseconomies in foreign expansion. *Journal of World Business*. doi: 10. 1016/j. jwb. 2013. 02. 003.

Johanson, J. & Vahlne, J. E. 1977. Internationalization process of the firm—A model of knowledge development and increasing foreign market commitments. *Journal of International Business Studies*, 8(1): 23 – 32.

Johanson, J. & Vahlne, J. E. 2009. The Uppsala internationalization process model revisited: From liability of foreignness to liability of outsidership. *Journal of International Business Studies*, 40(9): 1411 – 1431.

Jones, G. R. & Hill, C. W. 1988. Transaction cost analysis of strategy – structure choice. *Strategic Management Journal*, 9(2): 159 – 172.

Kim, W. C. Hwang, P. , & Burgers, W. P. 1993. Multinationals' diversification and the risk–return trade–off. *Strategic Management Journal*, 14(4): 275 – 286.

Knight, G. A. & Cavusgil, S. T. 2004. Innovation, organizational capabilities, and the born – global firm. *Journal of International Business Studies*, 35(2): 124 – 141.

Kogut, B. & Zander, U. 1992. Knowledge of the firm, combinative capabilities, and the replication of technology. *Organization Science*, 3(3): 383 – 397.

Kogut, B. & Zander, U. 1993. Knowledge of the firm and the evolutionary—Theory of the multinational – corporation. *Journal of International Business Studies*, 24(4): 625 – 645.

Kuemmerle, W. 1999. The drivers of foreign direct investment into research and development: An empirical investigation. *Journal of International Business Studies*, 30(1): 1 – 24.

Kuemmerle, W. 2002. Home base and knowledge management in international ventures. *Journal of Business Venturing*, 17(2): 99 – 122.

Kumaraswamy, A. Mudambi, R. , Saranga, H. , & Tripathy, A. 2012. Catch – up strategies in the Indian auto components industry: Domestic firms' responses to market liberalization. *Journal of International Business Studies*, 43(4): 368 – 395.

Lamin, A. & Livanis, G. 2013. Agglomeration, catch – up and the liability of foreignness in emerging economies. *Journal of International Business Studies*, 44(6): 579 – 606.

Lane, P. J. & Lubatkin, M. 1998. Relative absorptive capacity and interorganizational learning. *Strategic Management Journal*, 19(5): 461 –477.

Lecraw, D. J. 1983. Performance of transnational corporations in less developed countries. *Journal of International Business Studies*,14(1): 15 –33.

Levinthal, D. A. & March, J. G. 1993. The myopia of learning. *Strategic Management Journal*, 14(S2): 95 –112.

Levitt, B. & March, J. G. 1988. Organizational learning. *Annual Review of Sociology*, 14: 319 –340.

Li, J. (2013) The internationalization of entrepreneurial firms from emerging economies: The roles of institutional transitions and market opportunities. *Journal of International Entrepreneurship*, 11: 158 –171

Li, H. Y. & Atuahene – Gima, K. 2001. Product innovation strategy and the performance of new technology ventures in China. *Academy of Management Journal*, 44 (6): 1123 –1134.

Li, J., Chen, D. & Shapiro, D. M. 2010. Product innovations in emerging economies: The role of foreign knowledge access channels and internal efforts in Chinese firms. *Management and Organization Review*, 6(2): 243 –266.

Li, J. & Kozhikode, R. K. 2008. Knowledge management and innovation strategy: The challenge for latecomers in emerging economies. *Asia Pacific Journal of Management*, 25(3): 429 –450.

Lu, J. W. & Beamish, P. W. 2004. International diversification and firm performance: The S – curve hypothesis. *Academy of Management Journal*, 47(4): 598 –609.

Luo, Y. D. Sun, J. Y., & Wang, S. L. 2011. Emerging economy copycats: Capability, environment, and strategy. *Academy of Management Perspectives*, 25(2): 37 –56.

Luo, Y. D. & Tung, R. L. 2007. International expansion of emerging market enterprises: A springboard perspective. *Journal of International Business Studies*, 38 (4): 481 –498.

Lyles, M. A. & Salk, J. E. 1996. Knowledge acquisition from foreign parents in international joint ventures: An empirical examination in the Hungarian context. *Journal of International Business Studies*, 27(5): 877 –903.

Makino, S. & Delios, A. 1996. Local knowledge transfer and performance: Implications for alliance formation in Asia. *Journal of International Business Studies*, 27(5): 905 –927.

March, J. G. 1991. Exploration and exploitation in organizational learning. *Organization Science*, 2(1): 71 –87.

Mathews, J. A. & Cho, D. S. 1999. Combinative capabilities and organizational learning in latecomer firms: The case of the Korean semiconductor industry. *Journal of World Business*, 34(2): 139 –156.

Meyer, K. & Thaijongrak, O. 2012. The dynamics of emerging economy MNEs: How the internationalization process model can guide future research. *Asia Pacific Journal of Management*. doi:10. 1007/s10490 – 012 – 9313 – 9

Nelson, R. 1993. *National innovation systems: A comparative analysis*. New York:Oxford University Press.

Nunnally, J. C. 1978. *Psychometric Theory*. New York: McGraw – Hill.

Peng, M. W. 2003. Institutional transitions and strategic choices. *Academy of Management Review*, 28(2): 275 – 296.

Peng, M. W. & Luo, Y. D. 2000. Managerial ties and firm performance in a transition economy: The nature of a micro – macro link. *Academy of Management Journal*, 43 (3): 486 – 501.

Penrose, E. T. 1995. *The Theory of Grow of the Firm*. New York: Oxford University Press.

Petersen, B. , Pedersen, T. & Lyles, M. A. 2008. Closing knowledge gaps in foreign markets. *Journal of International Business Studies*, 39(7): 1097 – 1113.

Schumpeter, J. A. & Opie, R. 1955. *The theory of economic development: An inquiry into profits, capital, credit, interest, and the business cycle, from the German*. Boston: Harvard University Press.

Sim, A. & Pandian, J. R. 2003. Emerging Asian MNEs and their internationalization strategies—Case study evidence on Taiwanese and Singaporean firms. *Asia Pacific Journal of Management*, 20(1): 27 – 50.

Tsao, S. M. & Chen, G. Z. 2012. The impact of internationalization on performance and innovation: The moderating effects of ownership concentration. *Asia Pacific Journal of Management*, 29(3): 617 – 642.

Vermeulen, F. & Barkema, H. 2002. Pace, rhythm, and scope: Process dependence in building a profitable multinational corporation. *Strategic Management Journal*, 23 (7): 637 – 653.

Wales, W. J. , Parida, V. , & Patel, P. C. 2013. Too much of a good thing? Absorptive capacity, firm performance, and the moderating role of entrepreneurial orientation. *Strategic Management Journal*, 34(5): 622 – 633.

Walsh, J. P. 1995. Managerial and organizational cognition: Notes from a trip down memory lane. *Organization Science*, 6(3): 280 – 321.

Wanous, J. P. & Youtz, M. A. 1986. Solution diversity and the quality of groups decisions. *Academy of Management Journal*, 29(1): 149 – 159.

Williams, C. & Lee, S. H. 2009. Resource allocations, knowledge network characteristics and entrepreneurial orientation of multinational corporations. *Research Policy*, 38 (8): 1376 – 1387.

Yli – Renko, H. , Autio, E. & Sapienza, H. J. 2001. Social capital, knowledge acquisition, and knowledge exploitation in young technology – based firms. *Strategic Management Journal*, 22(6 – 7): 587 – 613.

Yli – Renko, H. , Autio, E. & Tontti, V. 2002. Social capital, knowledge, and the international growth of technology – based new firms. *International Business Review*, 11 (3): 279 – 304.

Zahra, S. A. & Garvis, D. M. 2000. International corporate entrepreneurship and firm performance: The moderating effect of international environmental hostility. *Journal of Business Venturing*, 15(5 – 6): 469 – 492.

Zahra, S. A. Ireland, R. D. , & Hitt, M. A. 2000. International expansion by new venture firms: International diversity, mode of market entry, technological learning, and performance. *Academy of Management Journal*, 43(5): 925 – 950.

Zander, I. 2002. The formation of international innovation networks in the multinational corporation: An evolutionary perspective. *Industrial and Corporate Change*, 11(2): 327 – 353.

Zanfei, A. 2000. Transnational firms and the changing organisation of innovative activities. *Cambridge Journal of Economics*, 24(5): 515 – 542.

Zeng, Y. P. , Shenkar, O. , Lee, S. H. , & Song, S. 2013. Cultural differences, MNE learning abilities, and the effect of experience on subsidiary mortality in a dissimilar culture: Evidence from Korean MNEs. *Journal of International Business Studies*, 44 (1): 42 – 65.

Zhang, Y. & Li, H. 2010. Innovation search of new ventures in a technology cluster: The role of ties with service intermediaries. *Strategic Management Journal*, 31(1): 88 – 109.

Zhang, Y. , Li, H. Y. & Schoonhoven, C. B. 2009. Intercommunity relationships and community growth in China's high technology industries 1988 – 2000. *Strategic Management Journal*, 30(2): 163 – 183.

Zhou, C. H. & Li, J. 2008. Product innovation in emerging market – based international joint ventures: An organizational ecology perspective. *Journal of International Business Studies*, 39(7): 1114 – 1132.

Zhou, L. 2007. The effects of entrepreneurial proclivity and foreign market knowledge on early internationalization. *Journal of World Business*, 42(3): 281 – 293.

个体—团队匹配对团队创造力的
影响及作用机制研究

杜娟[*]

【摘要】 21 世纪的商业环境变得日趋动荡,企业为了有效地应对这种不确定性,必须不断地创新,才能在"大众创业,万众创新"的时代谋取可持续的竞争优势。宏观层面的创新根植于微观的员工创造力。团队是知识经济时代企业管理的基本单元,因此如何培育团队创造力是企业面临的最紧迫课题之一。本文基于个体—环境匹配理论视角,开发了个体—团队匹配通过团队信息深度加工影响团队创造力的理论模型,并以制造业、金融业数家企业的 68 个团队为研究对象进行了问卷调查。多元回归分析结果表明:个体—团队匹配与团队创造力和团队信息深度加工正相关,而团队信息深度加工中介了个体—团队匹配与团队创造力之间的关系。

【关键词】 团队创造力、个体—团队匹配、团队信息深度加工

A Study on the Influence and Mechanism of
Individual – Team Fit on the Team Creativity

Juan Du

Abstract The business environment of 21 century advances amidst turbulence. In order to effectively cope with this uncertainty, enterprises should gain sustained competitive advantages through creativity in the age of "mass entrepreneurship and mass innovation". Innovation is rooted in employees' creativity. As team is the basic unit for business management in the knowledge economy times, how to nurture team creativity is one of the most urgent research programs. This article develops a theory model for studying individual – team fit effect on team creativity through deep processing of group information and the survey questionnaire is conducted under 68 groups of several

---

* 杜娟,上海外国语大学副教授,管理学博士,研究方向:人力资源及组织行为学。

finance and manufacturing enterprises in China. The results reveal that: Individual – team fit has a positive correlation with team creativity and the depth
of team information processing, and team information procession plays a mediating role between individual – team fit and team creativity.

　　Key Words　Team Creativity, Individual – Team Fit, Deep processing
of Group Information

1. 引言

　　进入 21 世纪,对于行业、企业,抑或对于个人而言,想要追求更光明
的发展前途,就一定要思考几个问题:如何才能做得不一样? 如何才能
做到更好? 当今社会,企业想要单纯通过模仿而成为行业的领导者是行
不通的,企业之间的竞争到如今已经演变为企业创造力、创新能力的竞
争,创造力逐渐成为领先企业的核心能力。企业通过创新可以获得巨大
的价值甚至精神回报,竞争优势的概念对于任何企业来讲早已不再局限
于企业的技术,而是企业能否在不断创新中前进,而这种创新能力又与
员工的创造力息息相关。毫无疑问,创新对于企业和个人的重要程度极
高,创造力这一概念既是创新的动力,更是创新的起点,正日益受到越来
越多企业的重视。企业若能激发员工的创造力,便可以获得更多更好的
产品、服务和流程。
　　到底什么是创造力? 创造力并不等同于创新。有研究者将创造力
定义为“在一个复杂社会系统中,一起工作的个人产生有价值的、有益
的、崭新的产品、服务、想法、程序或者过程”(施建农,1995)。可见,创造
力应当被视为创新的一个先决条件(Scott, 1995; Amabile, 1996),即必
要非充分条件,拥有出色的创造力并不能保证创新的实现,但创造力却
是创新的根基。国外学者在 20 世纪中期就开始了对创造力领域的研
究。最初该领域属于心理学范畴,直至 20 世纪 80 年代初期,创造力才
引起了管理学领域学者们的关注,但其焦点更多是在员工的人格特质、
心理特征和认知模式上,后来研究者才开始关注影响创造力的外部因
素。国内学者在西方研究成果的基础上,致力于探究中国背景下的创造
力。近年来,有部分知名学者也开始了对中国企业员工创造力的实证研
究(黄敏儿和马庆霞,2000),以及怎样开发员工创造力的研究(赵业和李
明岩,2004;孙恒有,2004)。
　　21 世纪的企业开始提倡以团队为核心的工作流程。同时,员工创造
力和团队创造力之间的关系基本也可以确定为既互相制约而又相辅相

成,团队创新的核心动力就是员工创造力,员工创造力也受到团队创新氛围的极大影响。因此,在当前竞争激烈的市场情况下,各类创新性企业应运而生,团队创造力的研究越来越受到重视。本文基于个体—环境匹配理论开发了个体—团队匹配影响团队创造力的理论模型,并且考察了团队信息深度加工的中介作用。本文的理论贡献主要有:第一,丰富了我们对于团队创造力的前因因素的了解。相对于个体创造力研究的百花齐放之态,团队创造力还略显单薄(Shally & Zhou,2008),本文研究个体—团队匹配对团队创造力的影响。第二,深化了我们对于团队创造力的前因变量的认识。个体层面创造力已经形成了系统的中介变量,如激励视角下的创造力自我效能感,认知视角下的创造性过程参与和情感视角下的积极情感。本文认为,团队信息深度加工是情境因素影响团队创造力的一个重要的中介机制。

2. 文献综述及理论模型的构建

2.1 文献综述

(1)个体—团队匹配

古今中外,众多学者试图给出个体—团队匹配的普适性解释,事实上,很多研究者都一致认为个体—团队匹配是人和所在团队相互包容的一种体现。Muchinsky 和 Monahan(1987)研究提出,所谓个体和团队的匹配,一是指个体和团队在观念上的互相包容,二是指团队通过薪酬等激励方式满足个体需求,同时个体又以个体的专有知识满足团队需求,是一个互相弥补的过程。Caplan(1987)等认为需求—供给与需求—能力两种认知大有区别,换言之,当个体和团队达成相互满足的情况下,易于匹配的发生。

值得注意的是,以往的研究大多只关注个体—团队匹配的一个特定方面,而缺乏具有逻辑性、全面性的个体—团队匹配研究成果。直至1996 年,Kristof 结合 Muchinsky 和 Caplan 两者研究理论之长,重新整合了他们的观点。Kristof 提出,个体—团队匹配产生的基本要求是个体和团队之间存在的差异较小,如所谓的"三观"、对待工作的态度等;当个体和团队存在资源上的互补特性,如个体以自身时间、精力和承诺满足了团队需求的同时,团队给予个体以财务上、物质上、心理上的满足,即产生互补匹配。他同时提出,团队凝聚力、成员归属感这些能直接影响团队绩效的因素都与这两种匹配息息相关。Chatman(1991)对这一观点进行了补充,其中涉及了个体—团队匹配对员工满意度的影响。

近年来,研究者又有了新的研究目标:如何有效地测量个体—团队匹配性。这个领域主要有两种观点:其一,直接测量;其二,间接测量。前者指员工自己对自己在团队中的适应性(匹配程度)进行评估;后者则是指通过测量个体和其所在团队的特征变量,再由研究者采用调查统计的方法进行综合评价。学术界普遍认为,由于直接测量的人为特性存在比较多,间接测量相比于直接测量更具有科学性和普适性。研究者们同时注意到,个体—团队的匹配性是具有动态特点的,无论是团队的人员流动、团队所处行业的调整,还是员工自身知识技能储备的变化,都会对这种匹配产生影响。

综上,一个工作团队若想提高个体—团队匹配程度,必须注重对员工价值观和工作目标的正确导向,甚至说是同化的过程。在创业团队中,这种以信念和目标为支撑的理念比比皆是,这种积极而又团结向上的企业文化,不仅对员工的创造力,而且对员工的信心和忠诚度都有着巨大的正面影响。反之,若个体与团队间的价值观、目标不一致,那么组织的投入便不能获得相应的回报,这种关系即为"准交易契约关系"。处于这种关系下的员工和组织的分分合合非常普遍。在我国,基金这一行业经理人的高跳槽率和离职率就是一个极其典型的例子。总而言之,培养员工去积极适应团队"三观"、使员工明确和团队一致的工作目标是企业提升员工和团队的匹配程度,进而提升员工忠诚度的有效方式之一。

(2)团队信息深度加工

综观信息加工领域的相关研究,学者们并没有将重心放在团队上。在这一领域具有代表性的研究者是 Hinsz(1997),他对于团队信息加工提出了富有建设性的模型。在 Hinsz 等学者们提出的这一模型中,我们可以清楚判别整个信息加工的过程。Hinsz 的模型建立依据是认知心理学,他在模型中明确了从目标、注意的过程到最后反馈、学习等阶段。处于同一团队中的成员们首先被给予工作目标,然后才会有团队信息加工的产生。注意的过程中,该模型主要考量的内容是员工的注意会如何受到同事、团队外部环境甚至团队规模的影响,成员们在平时沟通的过程中如何才能统一观点,当成员间信息不对称时他们又会如何处理等。Hinsz 采用本模型提出了团队信息加工的基本定义:团队成员间关于信息、想法及认知过程的共享和被共享程度,包括这种共享如何影响个体和团队水平的结果。事实证明,这一模型至少在西方背景下具有普适性,Hinsz 等的研究成功地解释了工作环境中团队信息加工的过程,且将其直观呈现在了人们面前。他的这一研究成果也成功区分了个体和团队信息加工的相同与差异,并为后来学者们找到了本领域继续的研究方向。

两年之后,Propp(1999)提出集体信息加工这一概念,在 Hinsz 的模型基础上尝试深化定义团队信息加工。该定义有两个潜在假设:第一,为了分享团队成员间的专有知识,成员间必须有信息交流;第二,团队中存在一定程度的共同知识,这对于团队工作是极有必要的。团队互动是找到这种共同知识及分享成员间专有知识的一种方式。集体信息加工这一概念表明了认知过程不再局限于在个体水平发生,也能在团队水平发生,这就涉及更深层面的假设和问题了。不过,Propp 的研究仍旧存在假设上的漏洞:他把团队成员专有知识和信息量的和等同于团队共有信息量,这个假设显然在正常情况下低估了团队信息加工的能力,即所谓的"超越个体认知之和"。此外,Propp 还假设成员的知识储备不会因为团队工作而改变,忽视了员工进一步深造或是互相促进的能力,亦即发生知识扩张的可能性。

为更准确地描述团队在信息加工中的认知过程,Gibson(2001)提出了四个阶段的模型:第一,感知、存储阶段,或是理解为一种积累的过程;第二,检索、构建阶段,或是一种互动;第三,协商、解释及评价阶段;第四,整合及行动阶段。这个模型很好地解释了个人信息是如何演化为集体信息的。Levine 和 Smith(2013)则提出了集体信息搜索与分布模型。该模型的主要观点是:第一,认知不仅在个体大脑中发生,更分布在个体、团队及工具中;第二,分析认知和动机间的关系,并在此基础上理解认知作为一种涌现的分布式过程;第三,团队成员自身和别人的信息评价能力会极大地影响团队成员的动机及认知间的关系,而这种影响又是由团队任务的性质所决定的。De Dreu、Nijstad 和 van Knippenberg(2008)的团队信息动机模型指出了自我和团队两种动机层次及两种动机类型:社会动机、知识动机。两者对信息的影响是不同的,社会动机影响信息性质,而知识动机影响成员们对信息的获取和加工深度。他们的模型把团队任务分为知识任务及判断任务,并且进一步探讨了高可论证性团队问题解决任务和低可论证性团队决策任务。这一模型清晰地向人们展示了个体动机类型和团队任务性质如何影响个体的信息加工过程,进而影响到团队的信息加工。

(3)团队创造力

早期研究中,团队创造力常与企业绩效挂钩。美国通用电气曾带头创建了"创造性领导者中心"(Center of Creative Leadership,CCL),用以开展团队创造力的相关研究。Amabile(1983)曾认为团队创造力与个人创造力本身没有区别。随着社会心理学的深入研究,团队层面的属性才逐渐得到普遍关注。团队内的相互作用产生创造性知识,团队为个人提供了更加适宜发挥创造力的环境,团队内的相互作用比个体的努力更加有利于解决问题。随后，West（2002）提出较为综合的团队创造力概念，认为团队创造力是在外部需求的影响下，通过一系列团队过程，将团队任务特征和团队知识、多样化及技巧转化为创造性的产品、工艺、服务或工作方式等的过程。由此可见，团队创造力的内涵正在由个人特征向群体合成特征转变。团队创造力并非个体创造力的简单加总，而是以知识和技能的共享、交叉、整合为重要手段，为个体创造了基于问题情境的互动空间，从而发挥出更大的知识协同效应和组合优势，使团队实现个体单独所不能实现的创造效能。

在团队创造力作用机理的研究方面，IPO 模型以"输入—加工—输出"的行为取向范式为主导，只解决了团队创造力的输入端或输出端的行为表象特征，却未能揭示"加工"过程的作用机理。近年来，随着认知心理学的兴起，逐渐形成了一种新的团队认知研究思路，将研究焦点放在促进团队协同合作的内隐认知的作用机制上，如信任、共享认知、集体理解、社会认知等，促进了团队创造力作用机理研究由行为表象向认知层面的深层转换。综上所述，基于现有的国外研究成果，国内关于团队创造力的研究仍处于初级阶段，中国情境下的团队创造力研究有待进一步展开。

2.2　模型构建及研究假设

基于上述文献回顾，本文构建了个体—团队匹配（Individual - Team Fit）、团队信息深度加工（Team Information Processing）和团队创造力（Team Creativity）这三个变量之间的理论关系模型，如图 1 所示。

个体—团队匹配　→　团队信息深度加工　→　团队创造力

图 1　理论模型

（1）个体—团队匹配与团队信息深度加工的关系

我们常说团队是否稳定取决于该团队内部是否和谐，而个体—团队匹配正是影响团队内部和谐程度的重要因素之一，若团队领导在选择成员时不经筛选，出现巨大的观念反差，后果往往是团队内部分崩离析。个体与团队匹配度的高低极大地影响着员工对团队其他成员的重视程度，并且是否会积极努力地维护和其他成员间的关系。Chatman（1991）的研究显示，这项匹配不仅影响团队的工作效率和工作观念，也会反过来对员工造成满意度和"三观"方面的影响。O'Reilly（1991）的研究也清晰地表明,个体和团队二者间对待工作的观念越是相似,越能促进个体的工作满意度,也越能促进团队内部成员间的信息分享和交换。这一观点得到了社会交换理论的支持,即当员工工作满意度高时,他会倾向于让本组织或这个团队中的其他人也感到满意。Muchinsky 和 Monahan (1987)曾提出,个体—团队互补匹配的重要因素是组织和个体的资源互补,稳定的个体—团队匹配能有效提高组织凝聚力,从而提升工作满意度。这正与 Hinsz 关于团队信息加工的模型不谋而合,只有团队的信息加工才能使团队成员共享个体不同的知识技能,而这种信息的加工正是建立在团队成员间相似的价值观基础之上的,因此,我们得到假设 1:

H1:个体—团队匹配与信息深度加工正相关。

(2)个体—团队匹配与团队创造力的关系

Muchinsky 在研究中指出,个体—团队匹配的一致性包含个体和团队在观念上的互相包容。根据社会认同理论和马斯洛需求论,自尊,或者理解为在团队中得到他人的认同,是人类生存的一个重要心理需求。换言之,当个体和团队间的匹配度很高时,成员的特质和团队的特质就具有极高的相似性或一致性。这样的工作环境促使成员去接纳他人、支持他人,并且团队内部更加和谐民主,这些情境因素都是非常关键的激发后天创造力的因素。诚然,员工个体先天条件能在一定程度上决定其是否具有创造力,即人格定义,但是目前越来越多的研究已经表明,创造力和员工个体能力、智力的相关性并不是显著的。我们有充分的理由相信,员工的自身条件优越与否只是一部分,想要发挥创造力,还与员工所处团队的情境和当前整体社会环境息息相关。个体—团队匹配度高的团队中,团队的心理安全感强,大家愿意群策群力,因此团队创造力就会高。由此,我们得到假设 2:

H2:个体—团队匹配与团队创造力正相关。

(3)团队信息深度加工与团队创造力的关系

对于团队信息深度加工和团队创造力的关系的假设,著名的创造力研究者 Amabile 早在 1983 年出版的专著 *The Social Psychology of Creativity* 中就有涉及这方面的概念。事实上,Amabile 在这本著作中一直强调要将创造力置于组织环境下,而不是脱离组织去研究。Amabile 认为,发生在团队水平上的信息深度加工较多存在于那些具有信息加工取向的团队里。Simonton(1996)提出,帮助者和角色榜样在发展创造性的天赋中起到非常重要的作用,这个帮助者的概念即团队中共同工作的成员,此处的帮助也具有多个层面上的含义,其中就包括团队信息的加工。普林斯顿大学个体与团队创造力研究小组的 Isaksen 等(2001)设计得到了与创造力相关的团体氛围的评价模型——SOQ(Situation Outlook Questionnaire），其中也包含了争论、设想支持、信任和开放性等与团队信息深度加工息息相关的因素。Hinsz 于 1997 年提出的模型清楚表明了信息加工的多个阶段，每一个阶段中，团队学习都贯穿始终。这种以团队为主体的学习形式和信息加工的模式，是以个体与个体间的信息互换为基础的。而团队创造力的产生，很大程度上正依赖于团队内部的信息交换为团队成员提供基于工作情境的互动空间，更使知识协同效应更为显著，发挥出更大的组合优势，实现团队中个体无法独自完成的创造效能。由此，我们得到假设 3：

H3：团队信息深度加工与团队创造力正相关。

（4）团队信息深度加工中介了个体—团队匹配与团队创造力的关系

Propp（1999）提出过一个相关概念：集体信息加工（Collective Information Processing，CIP）。该概念可以帮助我们看清团队水平的信息加工过程，并帮助我们做出团队信息加工在个体—团队匹配和团队创造力之间作用的假设。概念本身存在两个潜在的假设：第一，为了分享团队成员间的专有知识，成员间必须有信息交流；第二，团队中存在一定程度的共同知识，这对于团队工作是极有必要的。团队互动是找到这种共同知识及分享成员间专有知识的一种方式。这一概念向我们表明了个体在团队中的认知过程（包括信息获取、储存和检索等）不局限于在个体层面发生，也可以在团队层面发生。关于个体—团队匹配如何影响团队信息加工的问题，该模型也向我们呈现出了团队成员个体的知识是怎样演化为团队共有的知识，这种演化正是个体—团队匹配程度上的提高。团队中一定要存在好的个体—团队匹配使组织特性和个体期望相互结合，由此团队才具备良好的一致性和适配度。这种匹配显著提高了团队凝聚力，也使团队成员间的信息交换更加频繁，而这种信息的交换和再利用，即团队信息深度加工，会反过来作用于团队成员自身，使其愿意为组织目标的达成而付出更多的努力，同时鼓励团队成员不局限于过去的方式，积极进行创新，通过多种途径寻求更优的解决方案。在这种情况下，团队将会拥有较高的团队创造力。由此，我们得到假设 4：

H4：个体—团队匹配对团队创造力具有正向的影响，团队信息深度加工在两者之间起到中介作用。

3. 研究设计及变量测量

3.1　研究设计

本次研究在选取样本的过程中，以方便抽样为基本原则，选取了江苏、上海(上海为主)四家企业的员工进行访谈及问卷调查。在本次调研中,多样化的组织类型和产业类型有效地提高了外部效度,四家企业涵盖外贸、教育、银行和食品行业。本文所总结的访谈内容都是从这四家企业中的工作团队产生,所用的数据也是从这四家企业的 68 个团队共计 365 人中收集。参与本次调研的团队主要包括客户服务(业务)团队、销售团队、后勤团队和财务团队。本次调研的所有问卷都是现场发放,现场回收,问卷的总有效率为 100%。同时,把员工的理解能力和表达能力也纳入样本选择的考虑范围,因此尽量选择了教育文化水平比较高的研究对象,以确保研究对象能够相对准确、完整地回答我们的问题和完成问卷。

为了有效避免同源方差问题,我们采用不同的来源采集数据。具体地,员工填写个体—团队匹配和团队信息深度加工,团队主管填写团队创造力。

3.2 变量测量

为了保证测量工具的信度和效度,采用的量表均是在现有文献的基础上根据本文研究内容和目的进行修正而得到的,再通过查阅参考国内外学术文献,得到关于个体—团队匹配、团队信息深度加工和团队创造力的操作性定义及衡量方法。

通过 Cronbach's α 系数来测量量表信度,并使用 Lisrel 对关键变量进行验证性因子分析(Confirmatory Factor Analyses,CFA),得到对于研究模型的拟合评价。

个体—团队匹配:使用 Cable 和 Derue(2002)的量表来测量个体—团队匹配程度。由普通员工进行自评,该量表在本研究中的信度系数(Cronbach's α)为 0.847。验证性因子分析结果显示,$\chi^2 = 11.55$;$df = 13$;$CFI = 1.00$;$RMSEA = 0.00$;$NFI = 0.99$;$RMR = 0.08$。

团队信息深度加工:使用 Kearny,Gebert 和 Voelpel(2009)的量表来测量团队信息深度加工,由普通员工进行评价,该量表在本研究中的信度系数为 0.852。验证性因子分析结果显示,$\chi^2 = 105.78$;$df = 26$;$CFI = 0.90$;$RMSEA = 0.21$;$NFI = 0.96$;$RMR = 0.13$。

团队创造力:使用 Jia、Shaw、Tsui 和 Park(2014)的量表来测量团队创造力,由团队主管进行评价,该量表在本研究中的信度系数为 0.863。验证性因子分析结果显示,$\chi^2 = 104.87$;$df = 9$;$CFI = 0.92$;$RMSEA = 0.04$;$NFI = 0.94$;$RMR = 0.03$。所有变量都符合拟合指数的评价标准,研究模型与数据适配程度较高,拟合优度和区分效度良好。控制变量:选取的控制变量主要涉及被调查者在人口统计学方面的特征,可细分为

表1　相关系数

Variable	Mean	SD	年龄	性别	教育水平	工作年限	团队规模	任务复杂性	个体—团队匹配	团队信息深度加工	团队创造力
年龄	2.90	1.51									
性别	1.92	0.93	0.29*								
教育水平	3.01	1.05	0.33**	0.16							
工作年限	9.82	5.47	0.73**	0.29*	0.09						
团队规模	14.60	7.85	-0.26	-0.19	-0.21	-0.22					
任务复杂性	4.26	0.76	0.09	-0.01	-0.23*	0.06	-0.24				
个体—团队匹配	3.80	0.64	0.01	0.13	-0.17	0.04	-0.11	0.31**			
团队信息深度加工	4.92	0.60	-0.20	-0.30*	-0.34**	-0.27*	-0.02	0.09	0.39**		
团队创造力	4.30	0.82	-0.12	-0.20	-0.16	-0.19	0.05	0.32**	0.25*	0.36**	

注：①样本量=68；②*p<0.05 **p<0.01。

员工个人背景变量,如年龄、性别、教育背景、职位、工作年限等,以及相关组织变量,如所在行业、企业性质、团队规模等。

4. 数据分析

4.1　描述性统计分析

表1总结了变量的平均值、方差以及相关系数。分析表明,本研究模型的三个变量之间均存在显著的相关关系。个体—团队匹配与团队创造力正相关($r = 0.25$;$p < 0.01$);同时,个体—团队匹配与团队信息深度加工正相关($r = 0.39$;$p < 0.01$);团队信息深度加工与团队创造力正相关($r = 0.36$;$p < 0.01$)。研究的主变量:个体—团队匹配、团队信息深度加工和团队创造力之间的相关系数的绝对值最大是0.39,最小的也有0.25,并且所有的相关系数都是显著的($p < 0.01$)。

4.2　假设检验

本文采用了多元回归分析法来检验所提出的理论假设。从表2的数据中可以看出,模型2中剔除各个控制变量(年龄、性别、教育水平、工作年限、团队规模)的影响后个体—团队匹配程度对团队信息深度加工的影响是十分显著的($\beta = 0.53$,$p < 0.01$),也就是说,个体—团队匹配对团队信息深度加工有着正向的影响得到了数据支持,假设1成立;同理,从模型4的结果我们可知个体—团队匹配程度对团队创造力也有显著的正向影响($\beta = 0.37$,$p < 0.05$),假设2成立;从模型5的结果可知,团队信息深度加工对团队创造力有显著的正影响($\beta = 0.35$,$p < 0.05$),假设3成立;最后,引入中介变量,我们发现个体—团队匹配程度对团队创造力的影响变小($\beta = 0.31$,$p < 0.05$),说明团队信息深度加工在个体—团队匹配和团队创造力之间的关系中起着部分中介作用,假设4成立。

表2　多元回归结果

	团队信息深度加工			团队创造力		
	Model 1	Model 2	Model 3	Model 4	Model 5	Model 6
控制变量						
年龄	0.03	0.10	-0.06	-0.01	-0.07	-0.02
性别	-0.25	-0.15	-0.11	-0.04	-0.02	-0.02
教育水平	-0.33^{**}	-0.27^{**}	-0.25	-0.21	-0.13	-0.17

续表

	团队信息深度加工			团队创造力		
	Model 1	Model 2	Model 3	Model 4	Model 5	Model 6
工作年限	− 0.33	− 0.40	0.01	− 0.04	0.13	0.01
团队规模	− 0.20	− 0.10	− 0.04	0.03	0.03	0.04
自变量						
个体—团队匹配		0.53 **		0.37 *		0.31 *
中介变量						
团队信息深度加工					0.35 *	0.12
Overall F	3.60	8.68	0.70	1.62	1.21	1.40
R^2	0.33	0.60	0.09	0.22	0.17	0.22
R^2 Change		0.27		0.13	0.08	0.05
F Change			23.03 ***	5.75 *	3.49	2.95 *

注：①样本量 = 68；②*p < 0.05　**p < 0.01。

5.　结论

5.1　结论

本文主要对影响员工与团队创造力的主要因素以及个体—团队匹配对团队创造力的影响及作用机制进行了研究，并以制造业、咨询业数家企业的员工为研究对象进行了访谈和问卷形式的调研。研究的结果能帮助我们进一步理解东方文化背景下影响企业员工及团队创造力的因素，同时通过对问卷数据的分析也能看到个体—团队匹配与团队创造力和团队信息深度加工正相关，而团队信息深度加工中介了个体—团队匹配与团队创造力之间的关系。

影响团队创造力的因素可以划分为组织内部和外部两类因素：

从组织内部角度出发，组织结构、组织文化和人力资源都对激发组织的创造力起着举足轻重的作用。第一，组织结构。集权程度较低的组织对创新有着积极的影响，这类有机组织有着较高的灵活性和适应性，因此创新行为更加容易被接纳；资源分配相对较宽松的组织更能够负担创新行为所带来的费用和失败。第二，组织文化。受访者普遍认为创新型组织具有其独树一帜的组织文化，包括鼓励尝试、包容失败等，并且无论员工的创造力行为成功与否都能给予一定奖励。冒险和尝试组成该类组织的文化核心。第三，人力资源。员工在创新型组织中工作时，能够接受更多的培训和开发,并被给予较高的工作保障,再一次保证员工不必担心因犯错而遭到解雇。

而从组织外部因素来看,主要包括所处行业的市场情况和政治经济及社会环境。第一,市场情况。毫无疑问,企业的存活与否很大程度上受到市场环境的影响,尤其是产品服务市场中的供求变化。激烈的市场竞争往往激发组织成为更加适应市场情况的创新型组织,创造力成为了新的核心竞争力。第二,政治经济及社会环境。企业的管理哲学和理念离不开政治经济和社会文化因素的制约。随着企业经营规模的扩大、技术水平的提高,企业的管理理念和组织文化亟待更新,也就更加易受到当下的政府政策、法律法规、社会舆论等的监督和约束。

综上所述,员工创造力和团队创造力之间的关系可谓相辅相成而又互相制约。一直以来,员工就是企业赖以生存的基础和保障,时至今日,员工创造力更成为了组织创新的核心动力。与此同时,员工创造力亦受到组织创新氛围的影响。由此可见,现在的企业为了提高行业内的竞争力,应该积极建立创新型组织,培养具有创造力的员工和团队氛围。这样的工作团队应该有着鼓励冒险、接受失败的氛围,确保团队员工间信息的流畅性,并积极支持新想法,奖励勇于变革者。员工在这样的团队中工作时,也需要积极提升自我,其中包括:第一,协调个人目标和组织目标,努力使两方面的基调保持一致,从而实现自身价值最大化;第二,积极追求实现自我创造性的活动,当个人动机巨大时,根据研究表明,会极大提升个人的创造力;第三,保持好奇心,保持对新生事物的敏感性;第四,积极参与同事间的非正式氛围交流(即非工作时间的交流),相信好的点子能够在一瞬间产生。在这种交流氛围下,人的压力会比较小,从而思维更加活跃,易于从同事那里激发得到好创想进而演变为自身想法。总之,具有创造力的团队需要员工和组织共同的不懈努力。

5.2　研究局限和未来方向

第一,本研究数据是横截面的,尽管采用不同来源的研究设计,但数据可能存在一定程度的同源方差问题。为了加强因果推断,未来研究可以采用更加严谨的纵向研究设计或者实验研究设计。

第二,本文考察了团队信息深度加工作为个体—团队匹配与团队创造力的中介变量,但这可能是不全面的。个体—环境匹配认为,匹配是一个多维构念,未来研究可以进一步探究其他匹配形式(如个体—领导匹配)对团队创造力的影响。同时,匹配影响团队创造力可能通过其他中介机制,如团队创造性自我效能感、团队情绪氛围等,未来研究可以进行整合来考察哪个机制发挥的中介作用更强。

第三,本文聚焦于个体—团队匹配到团队信息深度加工到团队创造力的主效应,忽略了对情境变量的考察。未来研究可以继续考察团队领导以及团队氛围的调节作用。

参 考 文 献

Amabile,T. M. 1983. Social psychology of creativity: A componential conceptualization. *Journal of Personality and Social Psychology*, 43: 357 – 377.

Cable, D. M & DeRue, D. S. 2002. The convergent and discriminant validity of subjective fit perceptions. *Journal of Applied Psychology*, 87: 875 – 884.

Caplan R. D. 1987. Person – environment fit theory and organizations: Commensurate dimensions, time perspectives, and mechanisms. *Journal of Vocational Behavior*, 31 (3): 248 – 267.

De Dreu, C. K. W. , Nijstad, B. A. & van Knippenberg, D. 2008. Motivated information processing in group judgment and decision making. *Personality and Social Psychology Review*, 12: 22 – 49.

Gibson, C. B. 2001. From knowledge accumulation to accommodation: Cycles of collective cognition in work groups. *Journal of Organizational Behavior*, 22: 121 – 134.

Hinsz,V. B. , Tindale, R. S. & Vollrath, D. A. 1997. The emerging conceptualization of groups as information processors. *Psychological Bulletin*, 121(1): 43 – 64.

Jia, L. D. , Shaw, J. D. , Tsui, A. S. & Park, T – Y. 2014. A social – structural perspective on employee – organization relationships and team creativity. *Academy of Management Journal*, 57 (3): 869 – 891.

Kearney, E. , Gebert, D. & Voelpel, S. C. 2009. When and how diversity benefits teams: The importance of team members' need for cognition. *Academy of Management Journal*, 52: 581 – 598.

Kristof, A. L. 1996. Person – organization fit: An integrative review of its conceptualizations, measurement and implications. *Personnel psychology*, 49(1): 1 – 49.

Muchinsky, P. M. & Monahan, C. J. 1987. What is person – environment congruence? Supplementary versus complementary models of fit. *Journal of vocational behavior*, 31(3): 268 – 277.

O'Reilly C. A. , Chatman J & Caldwell D. F. 1991. People and organizational culture: Assessing per – organization fit. *The Academy of Management Journal*, 34 (3): 487 – 516.

Propp, K. 1999. Collective information processing in groups. In L. R. Frey, D. S. Gouran & M. S. Poole (Eds.), The handbook of group communication theory and research (pp. 225 – 250). *Thousand Oaks: Sage*.

Scott S. G. & Bruce R. A. 1994. Determinants of innovative behavior: A path model of individual innovation in the workplace. *Academy of Management Journal*, 37: 580 – 607.

West, M. A. 2002. Sparkling fountains or stagnant ponds: An integrative model of creativity and innovation implementation in work groups. *Applied Psychology*：*An International Review*，51（3）：355 – 387.

宝贡敏，徐碧祥．2006．组织认同理论研究评述．外国经济与管理，（1）:39 – 45.

郭德俊，黄敏儿，马庆霞．2000．科技人员创造动机与创造力的研究．应用心理学,6（2）:8 – 13.

施建农．2005．人类创造力的本质是什么？心理学进展,13（6）:705 – 707.

孙恒有．2004．企业员工创造力的激发．企业研究,（8）:58 – 60.

赵业,李明岩．2004．员工创造力开发策略．科学管理研究,（5）:95 – 97.

Qualities of Leadership Admired in China: From Two Imperial Concubines to Study of Leadership Attributes of Knowing Oneself, Knowing One's Circumstances, Dispelling Obsession

Zhenli Yao *

Abstract   An important characteristic of effective administration is successful coalition management. Effective presidents spend a great deal of time nurturing the support of internal and external interest groups vital to the success of the organization's goals. A Chinese idiom states, "Draw on the collective wisdom and absorb all useful ideas. Pool the wisdom of the masses." This article examines Xuan – zong (r. 712 – 756), a Chinese emperor of the Tang Dynasty, and looks at available information on his leadership style. Its methodology involves analyzing scholarly information and writing short interpretive accounts of this person's leadership abilities. Additional examples are given of Concubine Plum, Black Jade, Qu Yuan and Jia Yi. Leaders need to know whom to call when they need advice. It is critical that a leader build friendship with others in similar position. Professional networking strengthens a leader's ability to solve problems and keep informed on current issues. At the same time, the methodology used involves examining contemporary American writings on leadership in order that the famous Chinese people from history can be analyzed in the light of criteria set forth by American writers. The relationship of leader and follower is similar to that of close friends. The leader cares for, and is concerned about his subordinates; the follower repays the supervisor's kindness. In a harmonious relationship, both sides benefit. The Book of Changes (Yi – Ching) says, "When two persons are of one mind, their strength is sufficient, even to cut metal."

Key Words   Comparative Education, Cross – Culture, Leadership Attributes, Qu Yuan

---

  *　姚振黎,私立健行科技大学/中国台湾国立中央大学教授,研究领域为中国文学、教育政策、认知心理学等。

Qualities of Leadership Admired in China: From Two Imperial
Concubines to Study of Leadership Attributes of Knowing Oneself,
Knowing One's Circumstances, Dispelling Obsession   75

中国人欣赏的领导素养:从两位封建女性谈起到对自我认知、自知处境、消弭偏见的领导能力研究

姚振黎

【摘要】 做好结盟联合工作,对于一个有效的政府来说是很重要的。优秀的领导花费了大量的时间获取内外利益群体对自身的支持,这对于一个组织实现其目标而言至关重要。用中国的一个成语来说,就是集思广益。本文通过审视唐玄宗(712~756年),以探究其领导方式。本文的研究方法包括分析学术信息,解释说明唐玄宗的领导能力等。与此同时,本文还引述了梅妃、林黛玉、屈原和贾谊的例子。领导者在征询意见时,要有人可询。和身份地位与自己相似的人成为朋友对于领导者而言也很重要。专业的人际网络交流强调一个领导者解决问题的能力和知晓世情的能力。同时,本文还回顾了美国关于领导能力的作品,以便从美国作家的衡量标准来分析中国历史上的这些人物。领导者和追随者的关系就像朋友一样,领导者关照追随者,追随者则对领导者报以善意。如果领导者和追随者关系融洽,则彼此互惠。《易经》中写道:"二人同心,其利断金。"

【关键词】 比较教育、跨文化、领导属性、屈原

I have not penciled my willow – leaves – eyebrows for a long time;	柳叶双眉久不描,
The surviving cosmetics are mixed with tears to soil my red handkerchief.	残妆和泪污红绡。
Empress Chen of the Han did not comb and wash after she was discarded by her emperor,	长门尽日无梳洗,
Why do I need to get pearls from my emperor to comfort my solitude?	何必珍珠慰寂寥。

——From "A String of Pearls" by Concubine Plum (8th cent A. D.)

1. The History and Background of the Emperor with Two Concubines

After the imperial concubine Wu – hui passed away, Xuan – zong (r.

712 – 756), one of the emperors of the Tang Dynasty, assigned Gao Li – shi, his closest courtier, to go in person to visit all the beauties in the realm. After looking in every possible spot, the emperor eventually found Jiang Cai – ping.

Because the imperial concubine Jiang appreciated plum blossoms — the traditional symbol of nobility and purity for the Chinese — Tang Xuan – zong ordered his subordinates to build a garden and to plant plum trees in it for her special enjoyment. Henceforth, from the emperor to the lowest followers, everyone in court called her "Concubine Plum", instead of "Concubine Jiang".

The style of Concubine Plum was "quietly elegant, not gorgeous; tasteful and refined, not gaudy; abundant in graceful bearing and charm". Moreover, she was good at writing poems and painting, and at music and dancing as well. In a nutshell, she was a gifted lady. Xuan – zong had doted on her particularly for two years. But, the innate character of Concubine Plum was aloof and indifferent toward others. She controlled herself rigorously. Therefore, although she was gentle and cultivated, full of tender feelings, she could not satisfy the feeling of the emperor, whose character was always dissolute and unconventional.

When he met another lady, Yang Yu – huan, the new lover had a completely different style — "bright beauty that could yet be regarded as pure; dignity that could still be accepted as vivacious; elegance, but still with a little wildness." Yu – huan's vivaciousness and unruliness stimulated him and gave him a new lease on life. In the end, they fell in love, and Xuan – zong and Yu – huan became deeply attached to each other. No one, under any circumstances, could separate them.

Because of her eagerness to obtain this particular prize, Yu – huan had tried many ingenious schemes, and during the period of sentimental attachment testily demanded that the emperor choose between her and Concubine Plum.

Xuan – zong was definitely in a dilemma. Concubine Plum was the old lover, and Yu – huan was the new lover. The new lover rejected the old lover. Yu – huan was good at competing with others. Concubine Plum's character was to yield. Who could control the court? Who had the clear superiority? The answer was quite simple. The emperor suffered some discomfort by being forced to choose between two women at this time. He was of two minds, and

Qualities of Leadership Admired in China: From Two Imperial
Concubines to Study of Leadership Attributes of Knowing Oneself,
Knowing One's Circumstances, Dispelling Obsession   77

loathed to part from either one. The only person who could understand the
anguish clearly was Concubine Plum, who wrote the "Rhapsody of the East-
ern Loft" and "A String of Pearls" to express her feelings. The emperor felt
badly because the love – relation between him and Plum would no longer continue. His feelings were like a gnawing sensation deep within him. From that
time onward, he forsook his dawn – audiences and neglected state affairs.

Eventually, the revolt of An Lu – shan broke out in 755 and forced the
emperor to flee from the capital in Chang – an. Yu – huan, who had been
granted the title of Noble Concubine, died at Ma – wei Slope during the emperor's flight to Shu, in the Southwest. She was strangled by the emperor's
mutinous guards, who refused to go forward unless she was killed. Xuan –
zong found her death too ghastly to look at.

We can still read the famous historical narrative poem in Chinese literature that records the real, miserable, yet beautiful love story of twelve hundred years ago:

A little child of the Yang clan, hardly even grown,

Bred in an inner chamber, with no one knowing her,

But with graces granted by heaven and not to be concealed,

At last one day was chosen for the imperial household.

If she but turned her head and smiled, there were cast a hundred spells,

And the power and paint of the Six Palaces faded into nothing.

*The cloud of her hair, petal of her cheek, gold ripples of her crown when
she moved,*

Were sheltered on spring evenings by warm hibiscus – curtains;

But nights of spring were short and the sun arose too soon,

And the Emperor, from that time forth, forsook his early hearings.

And lavished all his time on her with feasts and revelry,

His mistress of the spring, his despot of the night.

There were other ladies in his court, three thousand of rare beauty,

But his favors to three thousand were concentrated in one body...

The Emperor's eyes could never gaze on her enough—

Till war – drums, booming from Yu – yang, shocked the whole earth

And broke the tunes of "the Rainbow Skirt and the Feathered Coat".

The Forbidden City, the nine – tiered palace, loomed in the dust

From thousands of horses and chariots headed southwest.

The imperial flag opened the way, now moving and now pausing —

But thirty miles from the capital, beyond the western gate,

The men of the army stopped, not one of them would stir

Till under their horses' hoofs they might trample those moth – eyebrows...

Flowery hairpins fell to the ground, no one picked them up,

And a green and white jade hair – tassel and a yellow – gold hair – bird.

The Emperor could not save her, he could only cover his face.

And later when he turned to look, the place of blood and tears

Was hidden in a yellow dust blown by a cold wind...

　　　　　　　　　　　—Excerpted from "A Song of Unending Sorrow"

　　　　　　　　　　　　　　　By Bai Ju – Yi(772 – 846)

　　　　　　　　　　　　　　(Translated by Witter Bynner)

The emperor became weak, old and ailing like a candle guttering in the wind. He was eager to look for another source of comfort and consolation when the Tang army returned to the capital.

He could not live without a trace of either Noble Concubine Yang or Concubine Plum. Originally, Concubine Plum had died at the hands of the mutinous soldiers a long time earlier. Therefore, Xuan – zong ruefully made use of Concubine Plum's portrait to comfort his loneliness. Meanwhile, he carved Concubine Plum's stone statue in order to commemorate that period of love.

In our life it is not often that the intricate fate of love runs smoothly. How could Xuan – zong predict that yielding to his feelings of love towards Yu – huan, would result in becoming further estranged from Concubine Plum?

Although his position was dignified and noble as an emperor, he still had no way out of the usual course of love. Moreover, people who are common citizens, such as us, are subject to the same fate.

On the other hand, love expresses human nature. It makes no distinctions between rich or poor, noble or humble.

2. Rule by Personalities in China, by Law in the West

We cited this tragic love story in Chinese history, because it points up a peculiarity of Chinese leadership, where the rule is personal. It is quite different when the rule is by law as in the West. In the U. S. , you have a complete system of law to protect everyone and decide everything, even when it is a trivial matter like chicken feathers and garlic skins (e. g. , the memo, "Animals or Pets in the VoTech Building at University of Minnesota").

I got a memorandum from the Department Chairman, Charles R. Hopkins, on April 7, 1995, saying,

"Several people have spoken with me regarding animals in our building. On the basis of their concerns, Barbara Pucel and I (Charles R. Hopkins) checked with appropriate University Personnel to determine whether any policies existed relative to the concerns expressed. We learned that there is a University policy regarding animals or pets in University buildings. Yesterday we received the attached document identified as Policy on Unauthorized Animals or Pets in University Buildings or on the Grounds. "

After reading it, from a Chinese point of view, the first impression was that it was funny. But later, it gives us such careful consideration to regulations. Everyone is equal, and is expected to obey the same rule. The goal of every policy is to make everyone have the same rights. On the other hand, a Chinese, even if he is wise, intelligent, and capable, if he has no chance to be promoted to responsible position by the leader, it is very difficult for him to put into effect his ideals. Consequently, to surmise what the leader's favor is the popular pursuit of those interested in officialdom as we are in the 21st century.

More than two thousand years ago, Han – fei – zi (3rd cent B. C.), the famous ancient Chinese philosopher, wrote the essay, "The Difficulties of Persuasion" to elaborate how difficult it is to surmise the intentions, or to serve the leader. The Chinese say, "To serve the leader is similar to waiting upon a tiger. " It describes so hard to please the leader. Han – fei – zi made clear his main theme from the very beginning, and wrote:

"On the whole, the difficult thing about persuading the leader is not that one lacks the knowledge needed to state his case nor the audacity to exercise his abilities to the full. On the whole, the difficult thing about persuasion is to know the mind of the leader one is trying to persuade, and to be able to fit one's words to it. "

"If the leader you are trying to persuade is out to establish a reputation for virtue, and you talk to him about making a fat profit, then he will regard you as low – bred, accord you a shabby and contemptuous reception, and undoubtedly send you packing. If the leader you are trying to persuade is on the contrary interested in a fat profit, and you talk to him about a virtuous reputa-

tion, he will regard you as witless and out of touch with reality, and will never heed your arguments. If the leader you are trying to persuade is secretly out for big gain but ostensibly claims to be interested in a virtuous name alone, and you talk to him about a reputation for virtue, then he will pretend to welcome and heed you, but in fact will shunt you aside; if you talk to him about making a big gain, he will secretly follow your advice but ostensibly reject you. These are facts that you must not fail to consider careful. "

Personal relationship and favorable or unfavorable turns in life are crucially important to whether a Chinese will be a leader. Therefore, whether you can become a future leader depends on whether or not you are favored by the present leader. We take this example of Xuan – zong's tragic love story as an illustration of this point.

From the point of view of Xuan – zong, who was more important for him, the leader, between Concubine Plum and Yu – huan? His masculine nature favored Yu – huan. Otherwise, the emperor would not have racked his brains scheming, or have spent so much energy, to "commandeer" his daughter – in – law.

From the point of view of the emperor, Yu – huan was not only beautiful, with a full figure, plump and smooth – skinned, and sexually attractive to suit the emperor's taste, but there were also some characteristics of her thoughts and disposition which were identical with Xuan – zong's is own:

(1) Yu – huan was vivacious and unruly, and could stimulate the emperor's aging vigor and vitality. It is possible that some men are not good at expressing their feelings, and their reactions are also slower. Therefore, when they meet a lady whose style is vigorous and a little unruly, her ebullient manner and warm words stir up their feelings immediately. The flirtatious statements make them have good communication and reactions. The emperor's amorous streak was touched. A sedate, shy character like Plum failed to see how to arouse him. It was easier to maintain a static relationship. The result between such different personalities would be lethargic and apathetic.

(2) When Yu – huan was feeling jealousy, she would quarrel and pester Xuan – zong, but at the same time she got his attention as well. It is worthwhile to go further into this point. Because most men are open to this ploy, even if they do not want to accept it, they can be overcome by it. From psychology we learn that some men appreciate women who go into hysterics, be-

Qualities of Leadership Admired in China: From Two Imperial
Concubines to Study of Leadership Attributes of Knowing Oneself,
Knowing One's Circumstances, Dispelling Obsession   81

cause most women of the hysterical type are showing their jealousy. Women feel uneasy or perturbed, owing to being afraid of losing their male companion. When women have a bad fit of hysterics, they cannot keep their temper under control. Under this situation, the men cannot bear to stand idly by. Quite the contrary, it will stir up the men's feelings of "being necessary and important". Even when the tears of a normal woman stream down her cheeks as she screams in a loud rage, it often makes a man cherish her and examine himself critically. Under stress, people often reveal their true feelings (If a lady has the intention to make use of this means to "control" men, it is definitely dreadful. But this is not relevant to this discussion here). Quite the opposite of Yu – huan's quarreling and thus getting the emperor's attention, Concubine Plum was too sedate, too restrained, and too yielding to act in such a manner. She would always withdraw to lick her wounds.

(3) Yu – huan could act like a spoiled child. She could also bewitch and be seductively charming. In Chinese philosophy there is too much of masculine principle, making this a male world. The competition of this man's world is so strong, that men live in a very stiff system, and face many different kinds of challenge. Moreover, only a man could hold the highest position to lead the state. When Xuan – zong retired to the women's quarters to take a break after handling political affairs, he needed to enjoy tender feelings. At this time, the women had to be tender and soft, coquettish and enchantingly beautiful. One was masculine; another was feminine. Of the two complementary principles in nature, the feminine is negative, the masculine is positive. Both of them need each other and are mutually beneficial, and should be in harmonious proportion. How could Xuan – zong let Yu – huan go?

Conversely, let us examine why Concubine Plum fell into disfavor. When she engaged in close combat, she made concessions; When Yu – huan was rude and unreasonable, or burned with anger, she yielded. She put up with many grievances, even when the emperor assigned Gao Li – shi to send her a string of pearls, she was still too stubborn, unbending, proud and aloof to graciously decline the emperor's kindly feelings. Instead, she wrote the following poem:

Express Chen of the Han did not comb and wash after she was discarded by her emperor,

Why do I need to get pearls from my emperor to comfort my solitude?

Actually, beyond the aloofness and arrogance, the poem transmitted her deep resentment and enmity. How difficult it was to divert herself from loneliness or boredom! At this time, although the emperor could have known how she felt, it was also difficult to put in more effort on behalf of Concubine Plum. At the same time, the subjective and objective factors had not permitted the emperor to take her part.

At that time, Concubine Plum was aloof and frosty in manner. Because of her appearance and gifts, the emperor certainly felt tender affection towards her. Without doubt, she was beloved by him. But, compared with Yu – huan's mind and character, her shrewdness and subtlety, it became a difference between austerity and warmth, indifference and enthusiasm, frigidity and sympathy. When the Prince of Han was careless and accidentally kicked Plum's embroidered shoe at the banquet, she was angry and walked out. She was in the sulks later, but Xuan – zong was unconscious of what happened. This is an example of her oversensitivity and pettiness. The emperor thought she was quite difficult, and tried to please her. Comparing the two ladies, Yu – huan liked peonies; Concubine Plum liked plums. For Chinese, the peony symbolizes riches and honor, wealth and rank. The plum symbolizes nobility and purity, proud and clean. It won't wallow in the mire with others. The characters of the two flowers accord with the dispositions and temperaments of the two women.

Although Xuan – zong was still in love with Concubine Plum and felt deeply attached to her, eventually, the real difficulty was that he diverted himself from loneliness and boredom, which ended in regret.

The reason we have spent so many words to compare Concubine Plum and Yu – huan is to demonstrate why a lot of talented people such as Concubine Plum are lonely and unused. Why was an appreciated and talented person like Concubine Plum out of favor? There are some Chinese proverbs, which are intended to comfort talented people: "The hero has to be capable of bearing loneliness. " "If some is not the object of others' jealousy, he is a mediocrity. " It is true, people will take a pessimistic view. Some of these personality problems are dealt with by the American psychologist, Erik Erikson.

According to Erikson, how we resolve the following eight crises determines who we will be:

Trust vs. Mistrust = hope or withdrawal

Qualities of Leadership Admired in China: From Two Imperial
Concubines to Study of Leadership Attributes of Knowing Oneself,
Knowing One's Circumstances, Dispelling Obsession   83

Autonomy vs. Shame, Doubt = well or compulsion

Initiative vs. Guilt = purpose or inhibition

Industry vs. Inferiority = competence or inertia

Identity vs. Identity Confusion = fidelity or repudiation

Intimacy vs. Isolation = love or exclusivity

Creativity vs. Stagnation = care or rejection

Integrity vs. Despair = wisdom or disdain

With all the power that the world has over us as we proceed through the early years of our lives, it is a wonder that any of us manages to resolve any of these crises in a positive way (Bennis, p. 62). If Concubine Plum could have been intimate, she might have replaced isolation; she could have been creative, to replace stagnation, she could have kept her integrity, to replace despair. In this way, she could have continued to be in the leader's good graces and thus change her tragic fate. Similarly, why do leaders who have talented people, still look for someone outside, the way Xuan – zong did in the case of Yu – huan? The answer is that the outstanding people always have their own judgment, and definite views. They have their individual character and personality as well. In addition, they have their own goals toward which they struggle. If the leaders cannot understand and respect them, the outstanding people will leave the leaders, and the really talented people will never be reluctant to be out of office. William James wrote, in *The Principles of Psychology*,

A man's self is the sum total of all that he can call his, not only his body and his psychic powers, but his clothes and his house, his wife and children, his ancestors and friends, his reputation and works, his lands and horses, and yacht and bank account. All these things give him the same emotions. If they wax and prosper, he feels triumphant; if they dwindle and die away, he feels cast down.

The leader begins, then, by backing himself, inspiring himself, trusting himself, and ultimately inspires others by being trustworthy (Bennis, p. 60).

3. Drawing a Lesson from the Novel, *Dream of the Red Chamber* (*Hong Lou Meng*) to Illustrate the Way of a Subordinate — Getting People on Your Side

The Dream of the Red Chamber, first published in 1792, is one of the greatest Chinese novels. Since the republican period (1911) Chinese fiction has absorbed some Western influence and developed in new directions. But even the finest of the modern novels cannot compare with *Dream of the Red Chamber* in depth and scope — it probes deeper psychological truths. To show his scorn for contemporary Chinese writing, a scholar versed in traditional literature would often ask, "What has been produced in the last eighty years that could equal *Dream of the Red Chamber*?"

Much partisan criticism reflects the inveterate Chinese habit of regarding *Dream of the Red Chamber* as primarily a triangular love story, and one, moreover, that could have ended happily. Bao – yu and his two girl cousins are physically attractive and enormously talented. But, we prefer to think of the novels as an excellent leadership parable. From this book one may learn how a leader can get together with his followers, and learn whether they are for or against him. One may also learn how the leader can keep the loyalty of his subordinates, and how a subordinate can accommodate to the leader, while still achieving his own political ideals.

Under this quasi – political reading, it seems such a pity that Bao – yu (the male leading role) and Black Jade (the female leading role), who are so ideally suited to each other, should have loved in vain. It is similar to a leader with a subordinate. Yet, if one examines the novel carefully, long before Black Jade is in danger of being rejected by her elders, she seethes with discontent. The elders are equal to a leader's brain trust, his aids and staff. Even in their carefree days, her every meeting with Bao – yu ends in a misunderstanding or quarrel, and these frequent quarrels are fraught with bitter and lacerated feelings. This is so because the two are diametrically opposed in temperament, despite the similarity of their tastes. Bao – yu is a person of active sympathy capable of ultimate self – transcendence; Black Jade is a self – centered neurotic who courts self – destruction. Her attraction for Bao – yu lies not merely in her fragile beauty and poetic sensibility but in her very contrariness — a jealous self – obsession so unlike his expansive gaiety that his love for her is always tinged with infinite sadness. Even if they marry, they cannot be happy in the romantic sense of the term; if Bao – yu continues to love, it will be largely out of pity — the kind of pity that Prince Myshkin showers upon Nastasya in *The Idiot*. Black Jade cannot break through all kinds of obstructions to become a suitable mate.

There are still other qualities needed by a leader, some of which are pri-

Qualities of Leadership Admired in China: From Two Imperial
Concubines to Study of Leadership Attributes of Knowing Oneself,
Knowing One's Circumstances, Dispelling Obsession   85

marily possessed by women. CBS executive Barbara Corday also works
through empathy, which she sees as particularly female: "I think women
generally see power in a different way from men. I don't have any need for
personal power, especially over people. I want to have the kind of power that
is my company working well, my staff working well. As moms and wives and
daughters we've been caretakers, and a lot of the caretakers in our lives were
women, and we continue in caretaking roles even as we get successful in business. And that feels natural to us. I have always been very pleased and happy and proud of the fact that I not only know all the people who work for me,
but I know their husbands' and wives' names, and I know their children's
names, and I know who's been sick, and I know what to ask. That's
what's special to me in a work atmosphere. I think that's what people appreciate, and that's why they want to be there, and that's why they're loyal, and that's why they care about what they're doing. And I think that is
peculiarly female. " (Bennis, p. 156)

Because Black Jade is obsessed with her own problems, she cannot get
people on her side at the same time. The leader or his right – hand man have
to draw a lesson from Black Jade, as a Chinese proverb says, "To take warn-
ing from the overturned cart ahead. " It is necessary to know oneself, to know
one's circumstances, and to get people on one's side. Otherwise, one will
be isolated, stagnated, and despairing.

Black Jade knows quite well that she does not have a powerful advocate
actively looking after her interests, but she would rather suffer alone than in-
gratiate herself with her elders. She is lean, tender, weak, soft in appearance, but in reality, she is aggressive, obsessive, and stubborn, even though
gifted. If she is at all a tragic character, then her tragedy lies in her stubborn
impracticality, in the perverse contradiction between her very natural desire
to get married to the man of her choice and her fear of compromising herself
in the eyes of the world by doing anything to bring about that result. For her,
to admit that she is indeed sexually and romantically vulnerable is to consign
herself to the greatest shame possible. She vents her emotions through negative acts of aggression, and in time her temper gets worse, her tongue more
raspish, and her manners more offensive. A tubercular invalid with few
friends, she then falls back on self – pity, thinking that she is indeed a pitia-
ble orphan with no one to plead her cause.

There can be no doubt that Black Jade exemplifies a type of beauty, clever, and talented. It makes our heartache to see such wasted talent. There must be some way to avoid her fate.

From the subordinate's standpoint, the thing that all men should fear is that they will become obsessed by a small corner of truth and fail to comprehend its over – all principles. If they can correct this fault, they may return to correct standards, but if they continue to hesitate and be of two minds, then they will fall into delusion. If we would be a leader in the future, learn to open our mind, and observe the individual character of the leader. Everyone's feelings, and tastes are different, just as their faces are different. We cannot guess by our imagination what the favor and though of a leader is.

Because we listen autobiographically, we tend to respond in one of four ways. We *evaluate*—we either agree or disagree; we *probe* — we ask questions from our own frame of reference; we *advise*—we give counsel based our own experience; or we *interpret* — we try to figure people out, to explain their motives, their behavior, based on our own motives and behavior.

These responses come naturally to us. We are deeply scripted in them; we live around models of them all the time. But how do they affect our ability to really understand? (Covey, p. 245)

Zhuang Zi (3rd cent. B. C.) was an outstanding philosopher in ancient China. One day, Zhuang Zi and his good friend Hui Shi were strolling along the dam of the Hao River when Zhuang Zi said, "See how the minnows come out and dart around where they please! That's what fish really enjoy!"

Hui Shi said, "You're not a fish—how do you know what fish enjoy?"

Zhuang Zi said, "You're not me, so how do you know I don't know what fish enjoy?"

Hui Shi said, "I'm not you, so I certainly don't know that you know. On the other hand, you're certainly not a fish—so that still proves you don't know what fish enjoy!"

Zhuang Zi said, "Let's go back to your original question, please. You asked me *how* I know what fish enjoy—so you already knew I knew it when you asked the question. I know it by standing here beside the Hao. "

Because Zhuang Zi was open – minded, he took notice of the outside world. It was quite different with Hui Shi, who was imprisoned by abstract logic. Therefore, Hui Shi could not understand the outside world, even though both were good friends, Hui Shi was obstinately clinging to his own

Qualities of Leadership Admired in China: From Two Imperial
Concubines to Study of Leadership Attributes of Knowing Oneself,
Knowing One's Circumstances, Dispelling Obsession　　　87

narrow point of view. No leader can afford to act willfully or insist on having his/her own way, like a solitary flower in love with its own fragrance. Some compromises are necessary. Go along with colleagues even in their "evil deeds", because "there are no fish in water that is too clean". People will have no friends when their character and morals are too noble.

Leaders need to know whom to call when they need advice. It is critical that a leader build friendship with others in similar positions. Professional networking strengthens a leader's ability to solve problems and keep informed on current issues. Whetten and Cameron (1985) state: "An important characteristic of effective administrators is successful coalition management. Effective presidents spend a great deal of time nurturing the support of internal and external interest groups vital to the success of the organization's goals. " (p. 462) The Chinese idiom is: "Draw on the collective wisdom and absorb all useful ideas. Pool the wisdom of the masses. "

Xi – men Bao (4th cent. B. C.), while Magistrate of Ye (in Henan Province), was clean and honest and had no self – interest even "as small as the tip of an autumn spikelet". He was, however, very indifferent towards the courtiers. Therefore the courtiers joined one another and together did him an ill turn. After one year of his term, he handed in his report on local finance; then the leader of the Wei State, Marquis Wen, took back his official seal. Thereupon he presented to the leader his own petition saying: "Formerly, your servant did not know how to be Magistrate of Ye. Now that your servant has learned the right way, may he petition for the seal in order to govern Ye again? If his work is again not equal to the official duty, may Your Highness sentence him to capital punishment with axe and anvil. " Marquis Wen, unable to bear dismissing him, gave him the post again. Bao, accordingly, imposed heavy taxes upon the hundred surnames and began to bribe the courtiers as promptly as possible. After one year he handed in his report. This time Marquis Wen went out to welcome him and even made bows to him. In response Bao said: "During the preceding year your servant governed Ye for Your Highness's sake, but Your Highness took away the official seal of your servant. This year your servant governed Ye for the courtiers' sake, but Your Highness makes bows to your servant. Your servant is no longer able to govern the place. " So saying, he returned the seal and took his leave. Marquis Wen, refusing to accept the seal, said: "Formerly I did not know you, but now I know you well. Please do now govern the place well for

my sake. " So saying, he did not accept the resignation. Xi – men Bao eventually found the "correct" way to serve and be satisfied with his leader, after
a period of time.

Qu Yuan (3rd cent B. C.), and Jia Yi (201 B. C. – 169 B. C.) are
other typical cases.

4. The Lesson from Qu Yuan — Dispelling Slander

Qu Yuan bore the same surnames as one of the royal families of the state
of Chu. He acted as aide to King Huai of Chu (328 B. C. – 299 B. C.).
Possessed of wide learning and a strong will, he was wise in affairs of government and skilled in the use of words. In the inner palace he deliberated with
the king on national affairs and the issuing of orders, and in the outer court
he received visitors and held audience with the feudal lords. The king put the
greatest trust in him, and the chief minister, who was thus forced to share the
same rank with Qu Yuan, vied with him for the king's favor and was secretly
disturbed by his great ability.

King Huai set Qu Yuan the task of drawing up a code of laws. While Qu
Yuan was still working on the rough draft the chief minister got a glimpse of it
and tried to get it away from Qu Yuan so he could steal the ideas for himself,
but Qu Yuan refused to give it to him. Thereupon the minister began to slander Qu Yuan, saying, "The king has given Qu Yuan the task of drawing up
laws, the sort of thing that anyone could do, and yet, when each new law is
finished, Qu goes about boasting of his achievement and saying that 'In my
opinion no one but myself could have done this!' "

The king, angered by these reports, grew cold toward Qu Yuan. Qu
Yuan grieved that the king should be so deceived in what he heard and that
his understanding should be clouded by idle slander, that petty evil should be
allowed to injure the public good and justice should be without a hearing.
Plunged into melancholy thought because of the affair, he composed his poem
entitled "Li Sao", which means "Encountering Sorrow". The historian, Si –
ma Qian (1st cent. B. C.) made the following comment:

*"Qu Yuan conducted himself with justice and forthrightness, displaying
the utmost loyalty and exhausting his wisdom in the service of his lord, and yet
libelous men came between them. This is indeed what it means to find one's
way blocked. To be faithful and yet doubted, to be loyal and yet suffer slander —*

Qualities of Leadership Admired in China: From Two Imperial
Concubines to Study of Leadership Attributes of Knowing Oneself,
Knowing One's Circumstances, Dispelling Obsession   89

can one bear this without anger? His will is pure and his conduct virtuous. Be-cause his conduct was virtuous, he chose to die rather than seek a place in the world. He took himself off from the stagnant pools and fens; like a cicada exu-viating from its shell, he shook off the filth that surrounded him and soared far beyond its defilement. He would not allow himself to be soiled by the dust of the world but, shining pure amidst its mire, kept himself free from stain. Such a will as his is fit to vie for brilliance with the very sun and moon themselves!"

Though Qu Yuan had fallen from favor and had been banished to Qi, in the northeast, he had anxiously watched the proceedings in Chu and had been gravely concerned for King Huai, never forgetting his desire to awaken the king to the danger that faced him. He hoped to be fortunate enough even-tually to enlighten his lord and reform the ways of the state. Repeatedly in his poems he expressed this desire to save the leader and aid his country, but in the end his wishes probed vain. He was unable to remedy the situation and eventually it became apparent that King Huai would never wake to the danger that awaited him if he journeyed to Qin, a rival state in the northwest.

Any leader, whether he is wise or foolish, worthy or unworthy, will in-variably seek for loyal men to aid him, and wise men to be his assistants. And yet the fact that we see endless examples of kingdoms lost and ruling families ruined, while generation after generation passes without showing us a sage ruler who can bring order to his country, is simple because the so-called loyal men are not really loyal, and the so-called wise ones are not wise.

A hundred years or so after Qu Yuan threw himself into the Miluo River and drowned, there was a scholar of the Han Dynasty named Master Jia Yi (201 B.C. - 169 B.C.), who was appointed as grand tutor to the king of Chang-sha (in Hunan Province). He visited the Xiang River and cast into its water a copy of his work, "A Lament for Qu Yuan".

From the actual persons and events mentioned above, we can learn the following lesson about leadership:

Every leader has to be on guard lest he be deceived in what he hears and lest his understanding be clouded by idle slander, and petty evil should be allowed to injure the public good. King Huai could not distinguish the true loyalty of Qu Yuan, and was misled by his own concubine, Zheng Xiu, and deceived in foreign affairs by Zhang Yi, so that he drove Qu Yuan from the court and trusted his chief minister and his son, Zi-lan, instead. The result was that his soldiers were driven back and his territory seized, and he lost six provinces to his enemies and died a stranger's death in Qin, the mockery of the world! This is the fate of those who do not know now to judge men! An ancient Chinese classic, the *Book of Changes* says:

Though the well is pure, men do not drink;	井渫不食,
My heart is filled with grief at it.	为我心恻。
If the leader is wise and will dip up the water,	可用汲,王明,
We will all share his blessings!	并受其福。
	——《易经》

The leader is the hope of his followers. If Qu Yuan was to achieve his political ideas, he had to adjust to the situation, and then proceed in an orderly way, step by step, to transform the situation. Let us examine Qu Yuan's leadership attributes:

When he reached the banks of the Miluo River was wandering one day along the river embankment lost in the thought, his hair unbound, his face haggard with care, his figure lean and emaciated, when a fisherman happened to see him and asked, "Are you not the high minister of the royal family? What has brought you to this?"

"All the world is muddied with confusion," replied Qu Yuan. "Only I am pure! All men are drunk, and I alone am sober! For this I have been banished!"

"A true sage does not stick at mere things, but changes with the times," said the fisherman. If all the world is a muddy turbulence, why do you not follow its current and rise upon its waves? If all men are drunk, why do you not drain their dregs and swill their thin wine with them? Why must you cling so tightly to this jewel of virtue and bring banishment upon yourself?"

Qu Yuan replied, "I have heard it said that he who has newly washed his hair should dust off his cap, and he who has just bathed his body should shake out his robes. What man can bear to soil the cleanness of his person with the filth you call 'mere things'? Better to plunge into this never-ending current beside us and find an end in some river fish's belly? Why should radiant whiteness be clouded by the world's bile darkness?"

It is worthwhile to think about of the fisherman's words. If you plan to be a leader in politics or business or agriculture or labor or law or education or whatever, "Do not stick at 'mere things', but change with the times."

Qualities of Leadership Admired in China: From Two Imperial
Concubines to Study of Leadership Attributes of Knowing Oneself,
Knowing One's Circumstances, Dispelling Obsession   91

This would be to take a passive attitude. A positive attitude would be to use your voice for change.

"Leading through voice, inspiring through trust and empathy, does more than get people on your side. It can change the climate enough to give people elbowroom to do the right things. When they use their voices among their peers, leaders improve the general climate as well as reshaping their own organizations to deal more effectively with the world. "

"The leader may discover that the culture of his own corporation is an obstacle to the changes he wants to introduce, because as currently constituted, it is more devoted to preserving itself than to meeting new challenges. " (Bennis, p. 167)

Robert Dockson had to change a negative climate when he arrived at CalFed:

"*When I came here, no one ever tried to teach me the business. It was a divided company, and it had factions with walls around them. They refused to speak to each other. I wondered if I'd made a terrible mistake. There were eleven senior vice presidents, and they all wanted my job. I decided that I wasn't going to clean house, which I was going to win all of them over, make them work with me instead of against me, and that's what I did.*

"*I think the first thing one has to do (in setting out to change a culture) is get people on your side and show them where you want to take the company. Trust is vital. People trust you when you don't play games with them, when you put everything on the table and speak honestly to them. Even if you aren't very articulate, your intellectual honesty comes through, and people recognize that and respond positively.* " (Bennis, pp. 168 – 169)

5. The Lesson from Jia Yi — Knowing Oneself

Jia Yi (201 B. C. – 169 B. C.) was a native of Luo – yang. By the age of eighteen he was already renowned in his province for his ability to recite the *Book of Odes* and compose works of literature. The commandant of justice, Lord Wu, who was at this time governor of the province of Henan, hearing of his outstanding ability, invited him to be one of his retainers and treated him with great affection.

When Emperor Wen (r. 179 B. C. – 158 B. C.) first came to the throne he heard that Lord Wu, the governor of Henan, was one of the most skilled administrations in the empire. He therefore summoned Lord Wu to court and made him commandant of justice. Lord Wu in turn recommended Jia Yi who, though still young, he said, had already mastered the writings of the hundred schools of philosophy. Emperor Wen accordingly summoned Jia Yi and made him an erudite. Jia Yi, only a little over twenty years old, was the youngest among the court scholars, but whenever the draft of some edict or ordinance was referred to the scholars for discussion, though the older masters were unable to say a word, Jia Yi would in their place give a full reply to the emperor's inquiries, expressing what each of the others would like to have said but could not put into words. The other scholars soon came to feel that they were no matches for Jia Yi in ability. Emperor Wen was highly pleased with Jia Yi and advanced him with unusual rapidity, so that in the space of a year Jia Yi reached the position of palace counselor.

Jia Yi believed that, since by the reign of Emperor Wen the Han had already been in power for over twenty years and the empire was at peace, it was time for the dynasty to alter the month upon which the year began, change the color of the vestments, put its administrative code in order, fix the titles of officials, and encourage the spread of rites and music. He therefore drew up a draft of his proposals on the proper ceremonies and regulations to be followed, maintaining that the dynasty should honor the color yellow and the number five, and should invent new official titles instead of following the practices used by the Qin. But Emperor Wen had just come to the throne and he modestly declined any ability or leisure to put into effect such far – reaching measures. He did, however, direct revisions in the pitch pipes and in the statutes and order the marquises to leave the capital and reside in their own territories, both of which measures originated from suggestions made by Jia Yi. Emperor Wen then consulted with his ministers, asking whether they did not think that Jia Yi was worthy of promotion to a top position in the government. Zhou Po, Guan Ying, and the rest of their group, however, all opposed such a move and disparaged Jia Yi, saying, "This fellow from Luo – yang is still young and has just begun his studies, and yet he is trying to seize all the authority in government and throw everything into confusion!"

After this the emperor grew cool toward Jia Yi and ceased to listen to his proposals, but instead appointed him as grand tutor to the Prince of Chang – sha.

When Jia Yi had taken leave of the court and set out on his way he

Qualities of Leadership Admired in China: From Two Imperial
Concubines to Study of Leadership Attributes of Knowing Oneself,
Knowing One's Circumstances, Dispelling Obsession   93

heard that the region of Chang – sha was low – lying and damp, and he feared
that in such a climate he would not live for long. Also he was aware that he
was being sent away as a reprimand, and he was deeply disturbed, since he
had left the care of power.

Afterwards the emperor appointed Jia Yi to the post of grand tutor to
Prince Huai of Liang. Prince Huai of Liang was the youngest son of Emperor
Wen. His father loved him dearly, and the boy himself was fond of literature, and it was for these reasons that the emperor selected Jia Yi to be his
tutor.

Several years after Jia Yi's appointment as tutor to Prince Huai of Liang
the prince was out riding one day and fell from his horse and was killed. He
left no heir. Jia Yi blamed himself for having failed to carry out his duties as
tutor properly, lamenting bitterly at the prince's death, and in a year or so
he himself died. He was then thirty – two years old. Let us examine Jia Yi's
mistake:

It is traditional that the Chinese respect the aged, and esteem the virtuous. Jia Yi was too young to understand the situation. ①He thought highly of
himself. ②He sought perfection, and was eager to fulfill his ideal in a hurry.
③He had hazy notions about the real situation. When the Emperor did not
assign him to assume an important position, he could not be patient. When
Prince Huai of Liang fell from the horse while riding, he blamed himself.
When we are in any circumstance, we have to realize who we are.

"The free ourselves from habit, to resolve the paradoxes, to transcend
conflicts, to become the masters rather than the slaves of our own lives, we
must first see and remember, and then forget.

"Obviously, we cannot do away with — or do without — families or
schools or any of the instruments of homogeneity. But we can see them for
what they are, which is part of the equation, not the equation itself.

"*Self – awareness = self – knowledge = self – possession = self – control = self –
expression.*"

"*You make your life your own by understanding it.*" (Bennis, pp. 70 –
71)

It is quite dangerous to "throw an egg against a rock" (i. e. , to court
defeat by fighting against overwhelming odds). Jia Yi's story teaches me, an
international student of state – financed studying abroad, who is a transient
guest, not to try to remain abroad. Therefore, even if I am at the American

church or the "foreign" fellowship group where everyone should be warmly accepting, I sense that I am ethnically different. By the same token, when the President of the private university poached me to offer deferential courtesy, I transfer my research and teaching from the national research – oriented university on invitation. I definitely do not disorganize the way of life ecology at campus. In spite of this, I am always humble and never take offense. Otherwise, it is like "an ant trying to topple a giant tree" (i. e. , ridiculously overrating one's own strength). Lastly, Jia Yi passed away when he was only thirty – two years old. His situation was like that of Black Jade who passed away when she was less than twenty years old. On the other hand, Emperor Wen of Han could not choose even the best person for the job, no matter what age. He was cowed into submission by the senior group of courtiers, and this resulted in Jia Yi's death when he was in the prime of life. The examples of Concubine Plum, Black Jade, Qu Yuan and Jia Yi lead us to the following conclusion:

From the leader's standpoint it is quite important to see things by himself without someone calling it to his attention. This is called "being clear – sighted"; and to hear things by himself, which is called "being acute"; and to make decisions by himself, which is called "being fit to lead all – under – heaven".

Once the King of Wei presented the King of Chu a beauty. The King of Chu was greatly pleased by her. His royal concubine, Zheng Xiu, knowing the King loved her, pretended to love her even more than the King did, and selected whatever she wanted of clothes or ornaments and gave them to her. The King remarked, "Zheng Xiu, knowing I love the new lady, loves her even more than I do. This is the way a dutiful son should support his parents, and loyal subjects should serve their leader."

Knowing the King never suspected she was jealous, the royal concubine purposely told the new lady, "The King loves you very much, but dislikes your nose. Whenever you see the King, always cover your nose with your hands. Then the King will love you forever."

Thereafter, the new lady followed Zheng Xiu's advice, and, every time she saw the King, would cover her nose. So the King asked his royal concubine, "Why does the new lady always cover her nose every time she sees me?"

"How can I know?" said the royal concubine.

Qualities of Leadership Admired in China: From Two Imperial
Concubines to Study of Leadership Attributes of Knowing Oneself,
Knowing One's Circumstances, Dispelling Obsession   95

The King kept asking her insistently. "Just a while ago," she said in reply, "I heard her saying she disliked to smell the odor of Your Majesty."

"Cut off her nose," said the King in anger. As the royal consort had instructed the coachman to carry out any order directly as soon as the King said any word, the coachman, accordingly drew out his sword and cut off the beauty's nose.

When we turn in the Bible to the *Book of Nehemiah*, there is a similar tale of attempted deception. Sanballat, the wily Satanic foe who tried to lure Nehemiah to Ono, near Lydda, some six miles southeast of Joppa, for the fifth time sent his aide to Nehemiah with the same message, and in his hand was an unsealed letter in which was written:

"It is reported among the nations—and Geshem says it is true—that you and the Jews are plotting to revolt, and therefore you are building the wall. Moreover, according to these reports you are about to become their king and have even appointed prophets to make this proclamation about you in Jerusalem: 'There is a king in Judah!' Now this report will get back to the king; so come, let us confer together." (Nehemiah 6:6 – 7)

Every leader has to remind him/herself, "Who comes here to tell tales, sows discord." In addition, he must not let himself be fooled by desire, or ambition. Nor should he be blinded by lust for gain. Greed is like a valley that can never be filled, and, furthermore, he will be swayed by his emotions. Anyone under the influence of his passions can hardly be pronounced firm and unbending. Moreover, a leader has to make decisions, manage conflict, and lead others to face the bright and hopeful future.

There has never been an enlightened leader who succeeded by keeping secrets from his ministers, but failed by being too frank with them. Similarly, there has never been an unenlightened leader who succeeded by being open with his ministers, but failed by hiding things from them, because an enlightened leader by definition attracts good ministers, and an unenlightened one by definition attracts bad ministers. If the leader of men is too secretive, then only slanderous reports will reach his ears and honest advisers will fall silent. Petty men will draw close to him and gentlemen will depart. *The Book of Odes* and "Dispelling Blindness" of *Xunzi* says:

"He mistakes darkness for light,

And foxes and badgers have their way."

This refers to a situation in which the leader is sunk in delusion and his ministers are evil. But if the leader is open with his ministers, then honest advice will reach his ears and slanderous reports will cease. Gentlemen will draw close to him and petty men will depart. Both of *The Book of Odes* and "Dispelling Blindness" of *Xunzi* says:

> "*Bright and enlightened are those below*;   明明在下，
> *Glorious and brilliant is the one above.*"   赫赫在上。

This refers to a situation in which the leader is enlightened and his ministers are transformed to virtue. Dispelling obsession is a task of top priority for every leader.

6. Conclusion

The relationship of leader and follower is similar to that of close friends. The leader cares for and is concerned about his subordinate; the follower repays the supervisor's kindness. The harmonious relationship will have regard for both sides. The *Book of Changes* (*I Ching*) says, "When two persons are of one mind, their strength is sufficient, event to cut metal."

Yan and Zhao were two small kingdoms in the Warring States Period (480 B. C. – 222 B. C.). The great kingdom of Qin wanted to destroy both of them. But Qin had not attacked them yet, and Zhao was about to attack Yan, Su Dai spoke to King Hui of Yan saying:

"Today as I came here I crossed over the Yi River, and a large mussel had just opened its shell to sun itself. Along came a heron to peck its flesh and the mussel closed up on the bird's beak. 'If it does not rain today or tomorrow, there will be a dead mussel here', said the heron. 'If he does not leave today or tomorrow, there will be a dead heron here', replied the mussel. Neither was willing to relax he grip, so along came a fisherman and bagged them both.

"Now if Zhao attacks Yan, Yan and Zhao will be able to hold each other off for a long while and exhaust their citizenry. I fear then that Qin will play the fisherman. May your Majesty please give this your most mature consideration."

"Good", said the king, and desisted.

When the mussel and the heron grapple, the fisherman profits — it is the third party that benefits from the tussle (*Zhan – guo Ce*). A Chinese proverb states, "If the lips are gone, the teeth will be cold." On the other hand,

Qualities of Leadership Admired in China: From Two Imperial
Concubines to Study of Leadership Attributes of Knowing Oneself,
Knowing One's Circumstances, Dispelling Obsession   97

if the leader and subordinate have a good relationship, they will achieve their ideals. My Chinese advisor has always told me, "If both of us cooperate, both will have benefit; if we do not cooperate, neither side gains. "Moreover, this sums up the relationship of leader and follower.

When KMT (Kuo Min Tang) had made a decision to change its legal 2016 presidential candidate, this behavior may be say to perpetrate a fraud. The excuse of KMT's leadership is Hong's policy of Chinese unification cannot be accepted by the common citizens in Taiwan. Actually, up to now the leadership of KMT is seizing power.

If a snipe and a clam are locked in fight, it is only to the advantage of the fisherman. DPP (Democratic Progressive Party) remains calm and takes campaign for election easily. For the leadership of KMT, with the skin gone, to what can the hair attach itself? While an oyster and a kingfisher were engaged in a bitter tussle, a fisherman (DPP) came along and carried them (leadership of KMT) both off. A thing cannot exist without its basis.

References

Bennis, W. 2009. *On Becoming a Leader.* New York: The Perseus Books Group.

Birch, C. 1965. *Anthology of Chinese Literature: From Early Times to the Fourteenth Century.* New York: Grove Press.

Covey, S. R. 1990. *The Seven Habits of Highly Effective People: Restoring the Character Ethic.* New York: A Fireside Book, Simon & Schuster.

Crump, J. I. Jr. 1970. *Chan - Kuo Tze* (The Intrigues of the Warring State) (2nd cent B. C.). Oxford: Charendon Press.

Erilson, E. 1982. *Life Cycle Completed.* Norton.

Hsia, C. T. 1968. (translator) *Dream of the Red Chamber.* New York: Columbia University Press.

Legge, J. 1815 - 1897. *Confucian Analects.*

Liao, W. K. 1959 (translator) *The Complete Works of Han Fei Tzu.* London: Arthur Probsthain.

Watson, B. 1968 (translator) *The Complete Works of Chuang Tzu.* New York: Columbia University Press.

Watson, B. 1961. (translator, Ssu - ma Chien, Shih Chi) *Records of the Grand Historian of China.* New York: Columbia University.

Watson, B. 1961. (translator) *Hsun Tzu: Basic Writings.* New York: Columbia University Press.

Watson, B. 1964. (translator) *Han Fei Tzu.* New York: Columbia University.

When Money Can't Buy Everything:
A Study of Multiple Bidder Cross –
Border Acquisition Auctions

Noman Shaheer   Sali Li   Yaqin Zheng *

Abstract   This paper studies cross – border multiple bidder acquisitions in which many bidders from different countries compete against each other for acquiring a single target firm. In an auction setting, highest price is expected to determine the victory of a bidder. However, our empirical evidence demonstrates that firms cannot win competitive auctions for corporate acquisitions just by outbidding their competitors. First, we employ transaction cost theory to map complexity, uncertainty and opportunity costs involved in cross – border multi – bidder auctions. Then, we argue that target firms reduce transaction costs by evaluating bidders on a number of factors besides price. We draw from knowledge – based view and institutional theory to pinpoint such nonfinancial variables. We find that relative neo – institutional distances between bidders and target decrease the victory chances despite high offer prices; whereas relative comparative institutional distance and relative bidders' prior experiences increase the winning probabilities despite slightly lower prices. So, corporations cannot successfully make international acquisitions just by paying large sums of money to the shareholders of target firms. Instead, they also need to overcome the liability of foreignness, earn legitimacy, and demonstrate relevant competencies to be successful in an international multiple bidder auction. Our paper is the first to introduce cross – border auctions in management literature and to empirically demonstrate the applications of transaction cost economics, institutional theory and KBV in this novel context.

Key Words   Multiple Bidders, Acquisitions, Institutional Distance, Economy Distance

---

* Noman Shaheer, Department of International Business, University of South Carolina, Cross – border acquisitions, PhD Candidate, nomanshaheer@ yahoo. com. Sali Li, Department of International Business, University of South Carolina, Multinational strategy & Cross border acquisitions, Associate Professor, sali. li@ moore. sc. edu. Yaqin Zheng, Department of Administration Business, Nanjing University, Cross border acquisitions & Cluster innovation, PhD Candidate, zyqqwb@ 126. com.

当有些东西用钱买不到的时候：
一项关于多投标人跨境收购拍卖的研究

诺曼·沙赫尔   李卅立   郑雅琴

【摘要】 本文研究不同国家的跨国投标人的收购行为,他们往往为了收购一个目标公司成为彼此的竞争者。拍卖的规则是,给出最高价格的投标人理所当然地获得胜利。然而,我们的实证证据表明,企业为了并购,不能仅仅通过抬高价格赢得竞争性拍卖。首先,我们采用交易成本理论来描绘跨国投标人拍卖活动的复杂性、不确定性和机会成本。其次,我们认为,目标企业会降低交易成本,评估投标人的一些价格以外的因素。我们从知识基础观点和制度理论来确定这些非金融变量。我们发现,相对较新的机构,投标人和目标公司之间的距离减少了胜利的机会,尽管投标人出价很高;而相对实力相当的机构和投标人相关的经验增加了中标概率,尽管价格略低。因此,企业不能仅依靠支付给目标公司股东一大笔钱就能成功地进行国际收购。相反,他们还需要克服外来责任,获得合法性,并展示相关的能力,以便在国际上多个拍卖中取得成功。我们的论文率先推出跨境拍卖管理文献和实证证明事务的应用程序,因为我们是基于经济学、制度理论和 KBV 的背景提出的。

【关键词】 多投标人、收购、机构距离、经济距离

1. Introduction

Cross – border acquisitions are imperative business practices in the corporate world and important pillars of strategic management and international business research (Dikova, Sahib & Witteloostuijn, 2010; Verbeke, 2010; Harzing, 2002; Seth, Song & Pettit, 2002; Hunt, 1990). Management scholars have extensively researched acquisition process (Very & Schweiger, 2001), cross – border acquisition strategies (Calori, Lubatkin & Very, 1994; Reur, Shenkar & Ragozzino, 2004), and determinants of successful completion of international acquisitions (Holl & Kyriazis, 1996; Dikova, Morosini, Shane & Singh, 1998). Yet despite this variety, most acquisition research mainly focuses on acquirers as decision makers of importance and little research is carried out to understand sellers' perspective (Graebner & Eisenhardt, 2004). Especially, given the fact that about 50% of acquisitions are made through multiple bidder acquisition auctions in which multiple parties compete to acquire a single target firm (Boone & Mulherin, 2007) and sellers enjoy the authority of selecting the final acquirers, understanding sellers' perspective becomes immensely important.

Current research, however, limits the role of sellers as price maximizing entities interested in highest dollar values (Jensen & Ruback, 1983; Aguilera & Dencker, 2012) and little strategic considerations. These notions were contradicted by Graebner and Eisenhardt (2004) who theorized acquisitions as courtships in which sellers, just like dating partners, are pulled toward attractive buyers who offer synergies, organizational rapport and long – term success of acquired enterprise, not just the dowry from marriage (i. e. , price or immediate financial gains). This courtship angle of corporate acquisitions can be particularly important in cross – border context because prospective acquirers from different countries and institutional backgrounds greatly differ in their respective collaborative potentials, and sellers evaluate price offers in conjunction with cross national similarities and differences to ensure future synergy. This is empirically evident from the fact that in approximately 1/3rd of international acquisition auctions between 1994 and 2013 reported by cross – border acquisition auction data by Securities Data Company (SDC), selling firms sold their businesses to low offering bidders.

Our paper intends to deepen the seller' perspective by examining the cross – border acquisition auctions. So far, a stream of research in finance has captured financial parameters involved in acquisition auctions (Bebchuk, 1982; Stout, 1990; Jennings & Mazzeo, 1991; Aguilera & Dencker, 2011). We argue that beyond financial concerns, there are deeply ingrained behavioral, managerial, and institutional aspects that will influence sellers' decision. We demonstrate this fact by being the first to introduce the impact of cross national factors (Johanson & Vahlne, 1977; Barkema, Bell & Pennings, 1996) and transaction costs (Coase, 1937; Williamson, 1979) on decisions making of selling firms. Moreover, the unique context of acquisition auctions helps separate buyers' and sellers' perspectives, and enables us to further extend the courtship theory to examine the multipartite dimensions of sellers' decision making. By doing that, this study sets up the broader stage for future research on acquisition auctions from strategy and IB standpoints.

Our research also significantly contributes to practice. We demonstrate that corporations cannot make international acquisitions just by paying large sums of money. Instead, they need to understand the perspectives of target firms, overcome liability of foreignness and earn legitimacy (Zaheer, 1995; Madhok, 1996; Kostova & Zaheer, 1999; Kostova, Roth & Dacin, 2008) to ensure synergies and collaboration. We hope that appreciation of sellers' perspectives will enable bidding managers to cost – effectively gain competitive advantage over other bidders without necessarily paying the highest price.

2. Theory and Hypotheses

2.1 Significance of Sellers' Perspective in Acquisition Process

Research on corporate acquisitions mainly centers on buyers as the decision makers of importance (Amburgey & Miner, 1992; Beckman & Haunschild, 2002). This focus on buyers' perspective has roots in theories of economic efficiency that claim asset transfer to the highest valuing owners (Schwartz, 1988). Accordingly, researchers predict an acquisition to occur if acquirer values an asset more than the target firm does (Carline, Linn & Yadav, 2011). That's why; the buyers' perspective, e. g. ability and willingness of buyer to pay higher prices, has been assumed to determine the outcome of acquisition process (Eckbo, 1983; Montgomery & Singh, 1987; Capron & Pistre, 2002; Laamanen,2007).

Graebner and Eisenhardt (2004) pointed out, however, that acquisition decisions involve consent of not only buyers but also sellers. They used courtship theory to argue that acquisition are just like marriages in which both buyers and sellers play an active role and sellers influence acquisition outcomes same as buyers do. An exclusive focus on buyers' perspective erroneously assumes sellers as passive entities who merely seek highest dollar values (Jensen & Ruback, 1983; Aguilera & Dencker, 2012) and exert little discretion over acquisition process. In reality though, sellers have important strategic considerations that go well beyond maximization of financial gains. That's why acquisition deals behave more like courtships that assign greater value to similarities and combination potential of dating partners, not the dowry received at marriage. Consistent with this analogy, sellers look for strategic factors like long – term synergies and future collaboration, not just price or acquisition premiums as assumed by buyer dominated research. Thus, a focus on buyers' perspective paints an incomplete picture and it is important to appreciate sellers' strategic decisions and long – term orientations for a comprehensive understanding of acquisitions.

Graebner and Eisenhardt (2004) set up a strong basis for further research on sellers' perspective. Unfortunately, their work was not followed up in subsequent literature partly because of difficulties in isolating seller's decision making process in acquisitions. Most of the existing acquisition research, particularly in IB and strategy, tends to focus on so – called negotiation acquisitions that are featured as being carried through mutual discussions between target firm and a single prospective acquirer. In such settings, it is difficult to parse out the role of sellers in the transaction, as it will be confounded by the buyer's role in reaching an agreement. This issue is particularly salient when using large archival datasets. Therefore, so far few studies are able to further extend the courtship theory developed by Graebner and Eisenhardt (2004) and to test the seller aspects of the acquisition in a large and more generalizable setting.

2. 2　The Context of Cross – Border Multiple Bidder Acquisition Auctions

Our paper advances research on sellers' perspective in acquisitions by examining how sellers evaluate bidders in acquisition auctions, a context that is novel in academic research but critical in business world. In contrast to the negotiation acquisitions, multi – bidder auctions acquisitions involve several prospective buyers extending price offers to acquire a single target firm and subsequently, sellers choose the final acquirer (Boone & Mulherin, 2007). This mechanism allows us to directly observe and test the selection and rejection of bidding firms by sellers and to examine major factors determining sellers' perspectives about bidders. Despite auctions are widely prevalent as historically about 50% of acquisitions have been carried out through acquisition auctions, little research in IB and strategy has explicitly examined this phenomenon. In finance and economics though, acquisition auctions are clearly distinguished from acquisition negotiations (Boone & Mulherin, 2007) and financial economists have excellently researched financial parameters involved in acquisition auctions (Bebchuk, 1982; Aguilera & Dencker, 2011; Stout, 1990; Jennings & Mazzeo, 1991). While acquisition auctions have deep financial roots, there are also subjective, qualitative, managerial and institutional aspects (Mintzberg, 1973) that can only be uncovered using management and strategy lenses. That's why, instead of combining negotiations and auctions in the same samples (as done by Capron & Pistre, 2002; Laamanen, 2007; Singh & Montgomery, 1987 to name a few), exclusive research on acquisition auctions can draw insights, for example role of sellers in acquisitions, which can inform both theories of management and phenomena of acquisition auctions.

The context of corporate acquisition auctions helps in distinguishing the decision making process of sellers from that of buyers. When multiple bidders compete for same target firm, the buyers' perspective is accurately reflected in their respective bids. On the other hand, the sellers' perspective is evident by the selection of ultimate winner. This choice of target firms sheds light on financial as well as strategic factors that shape sellers' decisions. The influence of sellers on acquisition auctions, particularly while selecting from internationally diverse bidders in cross – border context, is empirically evident from the fact that as opposed to predictions made by buyers' perspective led research; target firms sold their businesses to low offering bidders in approximately 1/3rd of international acquisition auctions between 1994 and 2013. Such decisions by target firms may cause distress and frustrations among highest offering bidders who value the target most, outbid their competitors by millions of dollars, but still fail to make desired acquisitions. That's why; we emphasize the need of further extending the work of Graebner and Eisenhardt, 2004 to better understand the sellers' perspective and multiple bidder acquisition auctions provide us an ideal opportunity.

Moreover, we also call attention to important but ignored phenomenon of multiple bidder acquisition auctions that has strong relevance to both theory and practice. Acquisition auctions are considered the most efficient selling procedures under typical assumptions (Dasgupta & Tsui, 2003) that generate 25% and higher acquisition premiums as compare to negotiations (Roll, 1986; Desai & Kim, 1988; Bradley, Betton & Eckbo, 2000; Bradley, Desai & Kim, 1988; Moeller, Schlingemann & Stulz, 2004; Betton, Eckbo & Thorbun, 2009; Bessler, Schneck & Zimmermann, 2015). That's why, under Delaware law (the predominant corporate law in the US), when a potential buyer makes a serious bid for a target, the target's board of directors is required to act as would auctioneers charged with getting the best price for the stock – holders at a sale of the company (Cramton, 1998). It indicates multiple bidder corporate auctions are pervasive enough to attract further attention from both managers and strategy scholars.

In this paper, we focus on investigating sellers' perspective in cross – border acquisition auctions. Our empirical focus on cross – border acquisition auctions is attractive because it highlights how sellers choose among heterogeneous bidders (Dasgupta & Tsui, 2003; Povel & Singh, 2006) coming from different countries and having diverse backgrounds. This heterogeneity among bidders leads to noticeable differences in collaboration potentials and synergies (Hymer, 1960; Hymer, 1976; Zaheer, 1995; Zaheer & Mosakowski, 1997; Kostova & Zaheer, 1999; Gatignon & Anderson, 1988; Lee & Caves, 1998) sellers expect from different bidders. Thus, cross – border context is suitable to identify main factors that differentiate bidders from each other and influence sellers' selection of and "ideal mate". Specifically, we will draw from exiting literature to outline how different perceptions of buyers and sellers lead to divergent valuations of price differences among bidders. Later, we will elaborate on courtship theory to develop hypotheses regarding strategic consideration of selling firms that moderate the sellers' valuation of price difference and influence sellers' selection of winning bidder.

2.3　Relative Price Advantage

Price, as reflected in target valuation and acquisition premium, has been considered the most critical determinants of the outcome of corporate acquisition auctions. From a buyers' perspective, there are strong theoretical reasons to believe that offering the most attractive financial deal significantly improves a bidder's likelihood of winning (Bebchuk, 1982; Aguilera & Dencker, 2012; Jensen & Ruback, 1983). Bidders in an auction primarily evaluate the feasibility of acquiring target firm as summarized hereafter.

First, buyers are interested in generating a positive economic value after accounting for acquisition premium and all transaction costs. E. g.

$$P1 < EV1 - TC1 \tag{1}$$

Where

$EV1$ = Economic Value received by Bidder 1 from acquiring Target firm

$P1$ = Price offered by Bidder 1 for acquiring Target firm

TC1 = Transaction cost of Bidder 1 for acquiring Target firm

As acquisition auctions are competitive contests, bidders cannot evaluate their economic values in isolation and need to examine their competitive position against other bidders. Participation of multiple bidders indicates creation of positive economic values for all bidders if they could acquire target firm on their respective offer prices and transaction costs. However, no bidder knows about the transaction cost of other bidders. Due to this information asymmetry, price becomes the only comparison point on which bidders can evaluate their relative standing against others. Accordingly, the best bet for buyers is to offer the highest possible price (Bessler, Schneck & Zimmermann, 2015; Capron & Pistre, 2002) in anticipation that higher price will lead to higher chances of winning the auction i. e.

To win the auction, P1 > P2   (2)

In other word, buyers who can generate the greatest economic value from acquisition tend to offer the highest prices to create highest values for selling firms and subsequently improve their likelihood of winning. Sellers are expected to maximize their gains from acquisition by choosing the highest offer and transfer assets to highest offering bidders (Schwartz, 1988). That's why, in multiple bidder corporate acquisition auctions, financial considerations, particularly highest price is expected to determine the victory of a bidder (Aguilera & Dencker, 2012; Walkling & Edmister, 1985). Acquirers are forced to offer greater premiums or run the risk of competing bidders entering the market in pursuit of the target (Bebchuk, 1982). Accordingly, we derive our baseline hypothesis:

H1 : *All else being equal, the greater the price difference between highest bidding firm and its competing bidders, the more likely it is that highest bidding firm will win the auction.*

Price carries undeniable importance. However, looking from sellers' perspective, price is not everything. While buyers take highest price as the best offer available to target firm, sellers evaluate not only offer price but also collaboration potential with prospective acquirers. This is because low synergy between seller and acquirer can result in higher transaction costs that jeopardize sellers' economic value due to two major reasons. First, acquisition process does not end with signing the agreement (Dikova, Sahib & Witteloostuijn, 2010) because after selecting a bidder, selling firms incur transaction cost of drafting, negotiating, monitoring and enforcing the contract (Coase,

1937; Williamson, 1973; Weitzel & Berns, 2006; Gatignon & Anderson, 1988; Lee & Caves, 1998). In absence of mutual collaboration (Chi, 1994), power struggles and conflicts pin down the value sellers makes from the trade (Wiliamson, 1975). The problem is so critical that 25% of acqui-sitions are abandoned after contract signing (Holl & Kyriazis, 1996), annul-ling any benefit selling firm makes by selling at high prices. Second, even af-ter post − acquisition integration, lack of synergistic combinations increases sellers' transaction cost by compromising the long − term prospects of new business (citation needed) and causing emotional, reputational and financial losses to selling firms (Graebner & Eisenhardt, 2004). That's why; target firms value synergy, combination and collaboration prospects to minimize the transaction costs arising both from uncertainty in contracting with selected bidder and from risk in future performance of acquired firm.

Similar to buyers, sellers evaluate acquisition proposals on the basis of both price and transaction cost. First, sellers are interested in generating pos-itive economic value (Hill, 1990; Chi, 1994; Chi & McGuire, 1996) which is possible if

P1 < EV1 − TC1

Where

EV1 = Economic Value gained by Target firm by accepting offer of Bid-der 1

P1 = Price received by Target firm by accepting offer of Bidder 1

TC1 = Transaction cost incurred by Target firm for accepting offer of Bid-der 1

Different from buyers though, sellers have the ability to evaluate prices as well as transaction costs it will incur with each bidder. Transaction costs do not have a significant influence on sellers' perspective if all bidders are homogeneous (Myerson, 1981) and offer similar combination potentials. In this case, transaction costs associated with all bidders will be same and it will be logical for sellers to focus only on offer prices. However, this homogeneity assumption may not be valid particularly in cross − border acquisition auctions in which bidders from different countries contest for same target firm. These differences in backgrounds lead to substantial heterogeneity among bidders re-sulting into noticeable differences in collaboration potentials and thus, differ-ences in transaction costs associated with each bidder. Some bidders create greater economic value for sellers despite relatively lower prices because of

higher collaboration potential and lower transaction costs and vice versa
(Dasgupta & Tsui, 2003; Povel & Singh, 2006, Graebner & Eisenhardt,
2004). That's why sellers comparatively analyze the price offers and transaction costs of all bidders and positive economic value is created only if

$$(P1 - TC1) > (P2 - TC2) \tag{3}$$

It indicates that despite offering higher prices, Bidder 1 may not create
enough economic value if its transaction cost is more than the transaction cost
of lower bidder (Bidder 2) and price difference created by higher bidder
could not account for this transaction cost disadvantage.

Table 1   Differences in Perspectives of Buyers and Sellers

Evaluation Criteria	Buyers' Perspective	Sellers' Perspective
Economic Value of Individual Bidder	$P1 < EV1 - TC1$	$P1 < EV1 - TC1$
Bidder Comparisons	$P1 > P2$	$(P1 - TC1) > (P2 - TC2)$

The differences in evaluation criteria of buyers and sellers, as summarized in table 1, distinguish the perspectives of buyers and sellers. While
buyers' perspective is mainly concerned with price differences, sellers have a
two – pronged objective. They are definitely attracted by price but simultaneously, they minimize transaction cost by seeking "ideal mates" who could ensure long – term success of acquired enterprise (Gatignon & Anderson,
1988; Lee & Caves, 1998; Kogut & Zander, 1992; Kogut & Zander, 1993;
Graebner & Eisenhardt, 2004; Hill, 1990; Chi, 1994; Chi & McGuire,
1996). While we have objective and quantitative data about offer prices,
there is no objective way of measuring transaction costs sellers expect to incur
with each bidder. Courtship theory, however, can help in estimating the factors that increase or decrease transaction costs for sellers.

The courtship angle of acquisition uncovers sellers' strategic, multidi-
mensional and long – term oriented considerations that influence perceived
transaction cost of sellers associated with each bidder. Sellers treat acquisition as a courtship in which partners aim at minimizing the "transaction cost"
(e. g. risks and uncertainties) by seeking commonalities in values, judge-
ments, attitudes and behaviors. Simultaneously, preference is given to cont-
enders with higher socioeconomic family background. Following the analogy,
sellers minimize transaction costs by selecting bidders from politically similar

countries who could offer better collaborative potential. At the same time, sellers tend to ensure future success of acquired business by preferring bidders from economically developed countries who could inject advanced expertise to acquired firm. Accordingly, we draw our hypotheses pointing towards sellers' tendency of ensuring smooth collaboration with acquirers and simultaneously securing strategic advantage for acquired enterprise.

2. 4 Relative Political Similarities

In this study, we conceptualize political similarities as the extent of resemblance among political institutions of different countries, as reflected in political stability, government size, democracy and trade bloc memberships. Similar political institutions tend to enforce similar rules across geographic borders which reduce variance among different political and regulatory environments (North, 1990; Rodriguez et al., 2005; Hall & Soskice, 2001; Whitley, 1999). This homogeneity subsides the negative effects of liability of foreignness (Eden & Miller, 2004; Kostova & Zaheer, 1999) for investors from politically similar countries by facilitating foreign firm's understanding of the local market and thus making it easier to interact with customers, suppliers, as well as target firms. It is similarly helpful for local actors, including target firms, to understand and collaborate with foreign firms (Salomon & Wu, 2014; Kostova & Zaheer, 1999).

Buyers from politically similar countries may significantly reduce sellers' transaction costs as compared to high offering buyers from politically distant countries. There are two major sources of sellers' transaction costs. First, transaction cost arises from uncertainty in contracting with selected bidder where any lack of mutual understanding leads to power struggles and conflicts between buyers and sellers. Second, transaction cost also arises from the risk in future performance of acquired firm as poor performance of acquired entity under new owner causes emotional, reputational and financial losses to selling firms (Graebner & Eisenhardt, 2004). Firms from politically similar countries, offers lower transaction costs to sellers on both fronts. With lower liability of foreignness and better understanding of host country environment, bidders from politically similar countries pave the way for smooth collaboration with sellers as well as long – term success of acquired enterprise. On the other hand, political differences between home countries of sellers and buyers result in differences among companies (North, 1990; Zhang & He, 2014;

Jackson & Deeg, 2008), which reduces collaboration potential and increases complexity, uncertainty and transaction costs (Berry et al. , 2010; Kogut & Singh, 1988; Brouthers, 2002; Brouthers, 2013; Anand & Khanna, 2000; Shleifer & Vishny, 1992; Zhang & He, 2014). Thus, firms from politically similar countries enjoy transaction cost advantage that enables them to create positive economic value for sellers against higher offering bidding contestants from politically distant countries.

The discussion over the impact of political similarities on sellers' perspective reinforces the difference in viewpoints of buyers and sellers. The uncertainties and complexities of dealing with politically and institutionally distant countries (Kostova, 1999) induce risk in future relationships between target and acquiring firms and thus, negatively influence sellers' perspective. Even if acquirer accepts risk and also offers the highest price among all competing bidders, sellers are sensitive to future success of acquisition and tend to select an "ideal mate" from politically similar countries. This fact was evident in acquisition auction of Unical Corporation (USA) in 2005 in which CNOOC (China) and Chevron (USA) contested. CNOOC offered $ 19.6 billion against Chevron that offered only $ 17.9 billion. However, uncertain about the future collaboration prospects with a Chinese SOE, 75% of Unical shareholders voted in favor of Chevron. The complexities, uncertainty, and risk of dealing with an SOE from politically distant China was high enough that Unical sacrificed $ 1.7 billion outright and chose the buyer with the best fit instead of going with the highest dollar value (Capron, 2004).

Enhanced collaboration potential is a major attraction that induces target firms to prefer prices offers by bidders from politically similar countries. A higher offer by bidders from politically similar countries add more economic value for sellers due to higher combination prospects and lower transaction costs. Thus, sellers favorably consider a higher offer only if it is made by bidders from politically similar countries. However, if tradeoffs are to be made, target firms favor low bidding firms from home or low distant countries against high bidding foreign firms from politically distant countries (Bugeja, 2011; Dinc & Erel, 2013).

H2 : The greater price difference between highest bidding firm and its competing bidders will increase the probability of the selection of highest bidder by selling firm only when the home country of highest bidding firm is politically similar to the home country of target firm.

2.5　Relative Economic Advancement

Second criteria sellers are interested is Economic advancement of the home countries of bidding firms. Firms from advanced countries enjoy certain advantages that are attractive for sellers. Sellers see acquisitions as a way to prosper through partnership and not as organizational death. Thus, they seek long – term success of acquired entity (Graebner & Eisenhardt, 2004; Larsson & Finkelstein, 1999) by selecting a competent partner. Buyers from advanced economies are better positioned to fulfill this criterion of selling firms.

Sellers highly appreciate and admire the benefits brought to acquired enterprise by buyers form developed countries. Mainly, companies from advanced economies garner greater capability, technological advancement and reliability due to the Economic advancement of their home countries. Thus, they can maintain competitive edge over local firms by exploiting home country specific advantages (Peng, 2003; Douma, George & Kabir, 2006; Tsang & Yip, 2007; Gu & Lu, 2014). These are exactly the characteristics sellers expect to infuse in acquired firms by selecting buyers from developed world. That's why long term oriented sellers tend to prefer the price offers by competent and reputable buyers from developed countries against higher price offers made by contestants from emerging economies.

Sellers also prefer higher collaboration potential with prospective acquirers and they perceive higher collaboration potential with firms from economically developed countries due to lower perceived psychic distance. As a country's level of economic development increases, the scope of its information infrastructure and the quality of its output tend to improve (Håkanson & Ambos, 2010). Thus, sellers can easily obtain relevant information about country and its companies, which facilitate sellers to better collaborate with buyers from developed countries due to lower perceived psychic distance and enhances sellers' perceived combination potential with bidders from developed world.

Sellers also reduce their transaction costs by selecting buyers from advanced economies due to institutional development of buyers' home countries. Strong institutions reduce transaction costs substantially (North, 1986, 1993; Anderson & Marcouiller, 2002), which makes bidders from economically developed countries more attractive even with lower prices. That's why sellers from developed countries with stronger institutional environments tend to do business with firms from other developed countries (Anderson & Marcouiller, 2002). Simultaneously, selling firms from economically less developed countries also prefer bidders from developed world because they serve as functional substitutes for incomplete development of formal institutions or institutional voids (Khanna & Palepu, 2006) helping target firms to escape from institutional constraints of their home countries (Hall & Soskice, 2001; Witt & Lewin, 2007; Luo & Tung, 2007). By the same logic, economically less developed countries suffer from a lack of institutional development (Acemoglu & Johnson, 2003; Acemoglu, Johnson, Robinson & Thaicharoen, 2003; Hnatkovska & Loayza, 2005; Loayza, Ranciere, Serven & Ventura, 2007; Loayza & Raddatz, 2007) that creates hidden transaction costs (Anderson & Marcouiller, 2002) and decreases the attractiveness of high bids made by firms from less advanced economies. Thus, due to lower transaction costs, sellers assign higher value to the price offers made by buyers from developed firms.

The discussion over the impact of economic advancement on sellers' perspective highlights an important distinction between viewpoints of buyers and sellers and reinforces the need of exclusive research on sellers' decision making process. From buyers' perspective, acquisition of firms in economically more developed economies (Cho & Padmanabhan, 1995; Zejan, 1990) is a utility – maximizing opportunity that grants buyers access to better resources and knowledge spillovers from local industry (Ambos & Ambos, 2011; Almeida, 1996; Manning, Massini & Lewin, 2008; Estrin & Meyer, 2004). Buyers from less developed countries prefer investing in advanced economies (Chen & Chen, 1998; Kumar, 1998; Lecraw, 1993; Makino et al., 2002) because it helps in learning from acquired firm and improving competitive position in home market (Tsang & Yip, 2007). So, buyers from less developed countries may have greater incentive than bidders from more advanced economies and accordingly, they may offer higher prices. However, seller's perspective is different from above mentioned buyers' perspective as sellers are interested in long – term success of acquired entity (Graebner & Eisenhardt, 2004; Larsson & Finkelstein, 1999) and buyers' goal of using acquisition as a tool to improve positioning in buyers' home countries is not appealing for sellers. That's why sellers sacrifice higher prices offered by firms from less developed economies. While buyers from less developed countries can still entice sellers with higher offers, greater economic development of home countries of certain bidders substitutes for higher bids by bidders from less developed countries. Greater the relative economic development level of the home country of a bidder, greater preference it will receive from target firm even with lower price offers.

H3 : *The greater price difference between highest bidding firm and its competing bidders will increase the probability of the selection of highest bidder by selling firm only when the home country of highest bidding firm is more developed than the home countries of competing bidders.*

3. Methodology

3.1　Data

The base sample for this study was obtained from the acquisition module of Securities Data Company (SDC) database, which provides detailed information about bidders, offer prices and outcomes of cross – border acquisition auctions. For the purpose of this study, a cross – border acquisition auction is defined as a corporate acquisition event with at least two interested bidders (Boone & Mulherin, 2007) whereas at least one of the bidders belong to a country different from the country of target firm. We constructed the base sample of target firms acquired through auctions by first compiling all bids made between 1994 and 2013. We excluded all auctions in which target firms and all bidders belonged to same country as well as all auctions in which no bidder could acquire the target firm. We ended with a base sample of 994 completed acquisitions that met our definition of cross – border acquisition auctions and had data available for bid prices and control variables. We removed all acquisition auctions participated by financial intermediaries because it was impossible to track the actual buyer in these cases. We also removed all financial institutions that were put for sales. We ended up with a sample of 400 auctions in which buyers and sellers were services and manufacturing firms. To measure the impact of institutional factors, we merged data with World Bank economic indicator database and Berry's institutional distance database (Berry, Guillen & Zhou, 2010). After accounting for missing values, we obtained our final sample containing 369 acquisition auctions.

3. 2   Measures

One novel feature of our hypotheses is that they treat acquisition auction as unit of analysis by simultaneously taking target firm and multiple bidders in an auction into consideration. Therefore, these hypotheses apply to both target firm and competing bidders involved in an auction. For ease of explanation, we treated highest bidding firm as the focal firm in the empirical analyses and coded all variables from the focal firm's perspective following precedent in prior research (e. g. , Tong & Li, 2013; Bessler et al. , 2015). As we are interested in competitive bidding and the differences between rival bidders, we calculated differences in all bidders' characteristics for all variables. The intuition is that, as stated by Bessler, Schneck and Zimmermann (2015), as the difference in important characteristics increases between rival bidders, the more likely will we observe a significant effect on the outcome.

Dependent Variable

Our dependent variable is the success of focal firm. Similar to previous studies on acquisition auctions, we treated our dependent variable as a binary one, which is coded 1 if focal firm (highest bidder) won the auction and 0 otherwise (Holl & Kyriazis, 1996; Bessler et al. , 2015).

Independent Variables

Our main independent variable is relative price advantage, which calculates the percentage difference between the price offers of two most relevant bidders in every auction, e. g. , winning bidder and highest price bidders. However, in cases where highest bidder was also winner, we used the price offered by second highest bidder. So, when highest bidder was not the winner, we calculated the price difference as

$$PD = \frac{Pa - Pb}{Pa} \tag{4}$$

Where

Pa indicates the price offered by highest bidder

Pb indicates the price offered by winning bidder

In cases where highest bidder was the winner, the independent variable was calculated as

$$PD = \frac{Pa - Pb}{Pa} \tag{5}$$

Where Pc indicates the price offered by second highest bidder

Moderators

To measure political similarities, we used the variable political distance from Berry et al. (2010) dataset, which uses pooled Mahalonobis distance formula to aggregate most important indicators of political similarities, e. g., political stability measured as the number of independent institutional actors with veto power within each host country from the Political Constraint Index dataset, the size of the government relative to the overall economy from the WDI and world and regional trade agreements information from the World Trade Organization (WTO).

To focus on the political similarities of bidders with target firm and to capture the relative advantage or disadvantage of bidders over one another (Bessler et al., 2015), we calculated the relative political similarities as the difference in political distances between competing bidders. We measured difference between the highest bidder and second highest bidder (or the winner) and to scale the result, we divided it by the political distance of highest bidding firm.

Consistent with the established practices (Kashlak, Chandran & Benedetto, 1998; Tsang & Yip, 2007; Beugelsdijk & Mudambi, 2013), we operationalized relative economic development by measuring the absolute difference in GDP per capita of highest bidder and second highest bidder (or the winner). We scaled this variable by dividing the absolute difference by the GDP per capita of focal firm and also winsorized the variable to reduce the effect of outliers.

The composite scores we created for independent variables and moderating variables indicated whether highest bidding firm was at an advantage or at disadvantage against other bidders. This helped us in capturing the impact of relative difference among bidders on the outcome of acquisition auction. Such techniques are widely used by in studies involving comparison of multiple parties across multiple characteristics (Tong & Li, 2013; Bessler et al., 2015).

Control Variables

We controlled for the effect of industry and year of acquisition as well as a number of variables that were found to influence the outcome of corporate acquisition auctions in previous studies. All these variables were provided by SDC database.

We first controlled for number of bidders that is found to influence both revenues and outcomes of acquisition auctions (Bulow, 1994; Slovin, Sushka & Polonchek, 2005). Next, we controlled for various deal level factors that can influence the perspectives of sellers about attractiveness of various bids. We controlled for mode of payment (Huang & Walkling, 1987; Fishman, 1989; Berkovitch & Narayanan, 1990; Slovin, Sushka & Polonchek, 2005) which measures whether payment was made in cash. The variable was coded 1 if payment was made in cash and 0 otherwise. This variable was measured as the difference between the mode of payment offered by highest bidder and the second highest bidder (or winner).

We also controlled the impact of past experience of bidding firms (Porrini, 2004; Aguilera & Dencker, 2012). This variable measures whether bidding firm had any incomplete acquisitions in past. For each auction, we took the difference between the number of highest bidder's past incomplete acquisitions and the number of second highest bidder (or winner) past incomplete acquisitions.

Deal attitude of bidders was also found to influence the auction outcome (Schwert, 2000; Officer, 2003; Bessler et al. , 2015). To measure bidders' attitude in takeover bid, we created a dummy variable coded as 1 if bid was unsolicited and 0 otherwise. This variable was measured by taking the difference between the highest bidder's attitude and the second highest bidder (or winner)'s attitude.

Finally, we took into account industry relatedness (Aguilera et al. , 2011) to control if acquirer and target firms are in same industry. We coded the variable 1 if the primary four – digit Standard Industry Classification (SIC) code of the acquirer coincides with four – digit SIC codes of the target firm, and 0 otherwise. This variable was also measured by the difference between the highest bidder's industry relatedness and the second highest bidder (or winner)'s industry relatedness.

3.3 Methods

To examine the interdependence between price advantage and probability of winning the auction, i. e. , to test *H1* , we used the probit model to estimate the probit equation with the dependent variable probability of success in auction and independent variable price difference. As the main independent variable is a binary one, we used the probit command in Stata with standard errors adjusted for 8 clusters in industry whereas we adopted cluster analysis to determine the groupings of data. Subsequently, the moderation by institu-

tional distances was examined as interaction between main independent variable and each of moderating variables. All independent and control variables
were legged by one year to control for reverse causality.

We tested the robustness of our results using alternative logit model with
robust standard errors using Stata 12. The results from both models were com-
parable. We have presented the results from probit model in this paper
whereas the results from logit model will be available upon request.

4. Results

Table 2 presents descriptive statistics and correlation table. Table 3
presents 4 models showing regression results.

Table 2　Descriptive Statistics and Pearson's Correlation Matrixa

	Mean	S. D.	1	2	3	4	5	6	7	8
1. Success of focal firm	0. 69	0. 46								
2. Relativeprice advantage	0. 16	0. 15	0. 02							
3. Relative economic advancement	−457. 5	13449. 7	0. 03	−0. 08 *						
4. Relative political similarities	1123. 9	1642. 3	0. 01	−0. 03	−0. 03					
5. Relative deal attitude	0. 15	0. 69	0. 27 ***	0. 06	−0. 00	0. 06				
6. Number of bidders	2. 11	0. 35	0. 09	−0. 08	0. 00	−0. 09	−0. 02			
7. Industry relatedness	0. 34	0. 48	−0. 003	−0. 03	0. 1 *	−0. 01	0. 05	−0. 04		
8. Payment method	0. 22	0. 42	−0. 03	0. 11 *	−0. 01	0. 09	0. 02	−0. 08	−0. 11 *	
9. Bidder's past experience	−0. 37	3. 58	−0. 26 ***	−0. 01	0. 05	0. 06	−0. 14 *	−0. 05	0. 01	−0. 06

Note: ^{a}n = 369　* p < 0. 05; ** p < 0. 01; *** p < 0. 001.

Table 3   Results for the determinants of the Success of Focal Firma

Variables	Model 1	Model 2	Model 3	Model 4
Constant	– 0. 42	– 0. 55	– 0. 51	– 0. 54
	(0. 59)	(0. 51)	(0. 51)	(0. 55)
Relative deal attitude	– 1. 44 ***	– 1. 43 ***	– 1. 43 ***	– 1. 46 ***
	(0. 26)	(0. 25)	(0. 25)	(0. 25)
Number of bidders	0. 36	0. 37	0. 37	0. 35
	(0. 35)	(0. 34)	(0. 32)	(0. 32)
Industry relatedness	– 0. 10	– 0. 10	– 0. 10	– 0. 09
	(0. 22)	(0. 21)	(0. 21)	(0. 21)
Payment method	– 0. 01	– 0. 03	– 0. 03	0. 02
	(0. 20)	(0. 20)	(0. 19)	(0. 19)
Bidder's past experience	– 0. 09 *	– 0. 09 *	– 0. 09 *	– 0. 09 *
	(0. 04)	(0. 04)	(0. 04)	(0. 03)
Relative price advantage		0. 53	0. 58	1. 28 **
		(0. 40)	(0. 43)	(0. 50)
Relative economic advancement			0. 003	– 0. 01
			(0. 003)	(0. 01)
Relative political similarities			– 0. 04	0. 02
			(0. 04)	(0. 04)
Relative price advantage × Relative economic advancement				0. 09 *
				(0. 04)
Relative price advantage × Relative political similarities				– 0. 34 *
				(0. 16)
Observations	369	369	369	369
Log pseudo likelihood	– 185. 5	– 184. 9	– 184. 4	– 182. 2

Note: [a]n = 369, Robust Standard Errors Appear in Parentheses, Standard errors are clustered by industry. Year and industry are included in all models.

$^+ p < 0. 10$; $^* p < 0. 05$; $^{**} p < 0. 01$; $^{***} p < 0. 001$.

In Table 2, Model 1 is the baseline model with control variables only. Only deal attitude and incomplete acquisitions of bidders achieve significance as controls.

Model 2 adds the main independent variable relative price advantage. Contrary to *H1*   , the variable is not significant although positive. Model 3 adds relative political similarities and relative economic advancement. The directions were consistent with expectations. Relative political similarities turned out to be negative indicating that more political distance will reduce while political similarities will enhance the chances of winning. Relative economic advancement turned positive indicating that bidders from economically advanced countries will have a higher chance of winning. Though, both variables did not achieve significance.

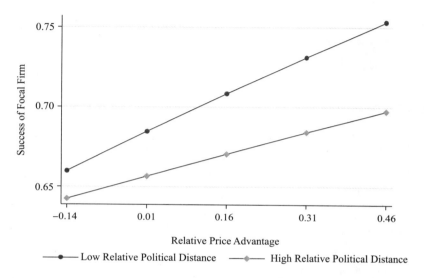

Figure 1   Interaction between Relative Price Advantage and Relative Political Similarities

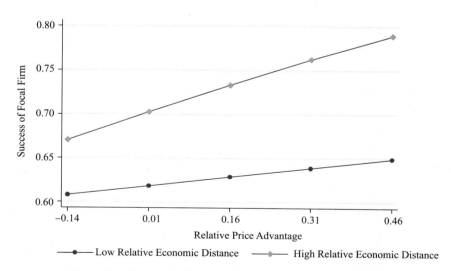

Figure 2   Interaction between Relative Price Advantage and Relative Economic Advancement

Model 4 is the full model with all controls, independent and moderator variables. Main variable, relative price advantage, achieved significance ($p < 0.01$) in full model. The interaction between relative price advantage and relative political similarities is negative and significant ($p < 0.05$) whereas the interaction between relative price advantage and relative economic advancement is positive and significant ($p < 0.05$) (see Table 2, Figure 2). Both interaction terms are consistent with *H2* and *H3*. Overall, *H2* and *H3* are supported; *H1* is not.

5. Discussion

The purpose of our paper is to examine sellers' perspective in the novel context of multiple bidder corporate acquisition auctions. We have extended the work of Graebner and Eisenhardt (2004) by highlighting the courtship – oriented nature of acquisition process. As opposed to mainstream research that mainly focuses on acquirers' perspectives, we have reinstated the significance of target firms as influential and active participants who use acquisitions to accomplish multiple strategic objectives, not to maximize immediate financial gains. In this endeavor, we have empirically demonstrated that the corporate acquisitions not only depend upon the wills and whims of prospective acquirers but also hinge on the viewpoints of sellers. Thus, we reinforce the critical need of treating corporate acquisitions as courtships by paying due attention to the perspectives of both buying and selling firms.

In our pursuit to discover salient features that influence sellers' perspective, we have generated some interesting insights. First, we did not find relative price advantages to be statistically significant predictors of the outcomes of acquisition auctions. This counter intuitive result may be explained from the perspective of both buying and selling firms. For buyers, it will be an inefficient strategy to outclass competitors in all areas and become a victim of winner's curse (Bazerman & Samuelson, 1983). A rational bidder with lower transaction costs is expected to take advantage of its strength by offering a price lower than the bidders suffering from higher transaction costs. In this sense, from sellers' perspective, higher prices may not be more attractive as compare to lower prices and final choice of seller may depend more on non – price related factors.

Second, we have made a conceptual contribution by introducing the role of sellers' transaction cost in acquisition auctions. We have demonstrated that sellers are sensitive to price as well as transaction costs related to each bidder. Institutional differences lead to low synergy and collaboration potential between sellers and acquirers which in turn magnify transaction costs arising from risk and uncertainty. Selection of an unfit bidder increases uncertainty as sellers face difficulties in contracting with selected acquirers and also magnifies risk in future performance of acquired business. That's why sellers seek to minimize transaction cost by selecting an "ideal mate" with highest collaboration potential.

Finally, our study has outlined how sellers' perspective about transaction cost is shaped by nationalities of bidding firms. We drew from Graebner and Eisenhardt (2004) courtship theory to identify national characteristics that have the potential of creating synergies and collaboration between buyers and sellers. Our findings about positive moderation effects of political similarities and economic advancement reinforce courtship analogy by proving that price matters for sellers only if bidders also offer complementarities and synergies needed for long term prospects of acquired enterprise.

Our study also offers valuable insights to management practitioners. We demonstrate that key success factor for bidders, particularly foreign ones, is not to overbid each other by offering higher prices. Instead, firms need to understand sellers' perspectives and earn legitimacy (Zaheer, 1995; Madhok, 1996; Kostova & Zaheer, 1999; Kostova, Roth & Dacin, 2008) in foreign countries to ensure synergies and collaboration with target firms. By demonstrating a good fit with sellers, cross – border buyers can gain transaction cost related advantage over competitors and can efficiently win the auction without making overpayments (Bazerman & Samuelson, 1983)[1]. By appreciating sellers' perspective, our paper facilitates bidding firms in understanding their relative transaction cost position in context of their institutional backgrounds and to efficiently win the auctions without necessarily paying the highest prices.

Besides empirical findings, the most important contribution of our paper

---

[1] Economically, the only exception to this claim arises when a bidder has so high asset specificity with target firm that it could not afford to lose the auction (Williamson, 1988; Capron, Dussauge & Mitchell, 1998). Also, uneconomic motives like national pride and managerial hubris can also lead bidders to inefficiently overbid (Hope, Thomas & Vyas, 2011; Hayward & Hambrick, 1997). However, such cases must be few and exceptional.

is introduction of the novel context of acquisition auctions as an exclusive venue for future strategy research. Acquisition auctions provide numerous opportunities that are not available while researching on negotiations. On most fundamental level, research on negotiations lack the presence of any comparison group for acquirers. As every acquisition case is unique in terms of future prospects, synergy potentials, industry sector and market values of target firms, it is unrealistic to combine many acquirers, from differently countries and industries in one sample to compare variables like importance of acquisition premiums. This inaccuracy is well addressed in acquisition auctions where accurate comparison groups are always available providing the opportunity of studying the acquisition process of same target company under same time frame against multiple bidders. It reduces noise in the sample and enables researchers to neatly isolate the variable in question.

Multiple bidder auctions also provide opportunities of better understanding the decision making of selling firms. As selling firms have clear alternatives and reference points (Northcraft & Neale, 1986), offer prices and transaction costs (arising from various institutional and firm level factors) are evaluated on a comparative manner. However, evaluation of multiple bidders coming from different and even unfamiliar countries, industries and backgrounds is a complex procedure. Due to bounded rationality, target firms cannot objectively analyze multiple offers and bidders to make rational decisions (Gatignon & Anderson, 1988; Lee & Caves, 1998; Markides & Ittner, 1994; Datta & Puia, 1995; Madhok, 1997; Simon, 1972). So, sellers' perspective is formed through subjective assessments that are influenced by opinions, perceptions, impressions and biases (Chiles & McMackin, 1996). In a nutshell, attractiveness of every bid lies in the eyes of target firms. This provides an excellent opportunity to analyze the relative importance of different variables in shaping sellers' perspectives, perceptions and even biases. Further adding to complexity, it is rare that a particular bidder could outclass all competitors in every aspect. So, study of cross – border multiple bidder auctions provide the opportunity of assessing the trade – offs made by selling firms while selecting the final acquirer. Researchers can analyze and even quantify the sacrifices made by target firms to reduce transaction costs and contract with favored partners.

Finally, acquisition auctions provide opportunity to analyze competitive forces involved in acquisition auctions. Empirical evidence suggests that buy-

ers pay higher takeover premiums in multiple bidder corporate auctions
(Bradley, Desai & Kim, 1988). While such statistics are motivating for selling firms, the competitive nature of acquisition auctions necessitates potential
acquirers to develop competitive strategies for winning corporate auctions at
lower costs. This tripartite tension among bidders and between target and bidders opens new venues for research like how firms gain competitive advantages against each other, how firms efficiently win auctions despite lower price
offers and what internal and external factors play for and against various bidders.

Overall, our paper has pioneered the examination of cross – border multiple bidder acquisition auctions from the lenses of transaction cost economics
and institutional theory. We have highlighted how subjective and qualitative
aspects (Vaughn, 1980; Kirzner, 1986; Pasour, 1991) complement rigorously calculated and objectively estimated financial parameters in understanding the outcomes of cross national acquisition auctions. That said, this paper
is just a humble beginning of a vast research paradigm. We have applied just
a few theories to identify only a limited number of factors important to acquisition auctions. These factors and theoretical frameworks are, by no means,
exhaustive. We just open a gateway for future research that will, we hope,
extend this body of knowledge by examining multiple bidder cross – border
acquisition auctions from perspectives of various management, strategy and IB
theories. This can help in capturing a series of relevant and highly crucial
variables that can inform existing theories, help bidding firms in gaining competitive advantages against other bidders and aid selling firm in overcoming
unwanted heuristics and making more economically efficient decisions. Taking advantage of extensive research by finance scholars on this topic and
using many available datasets on corporate acquisition auctions, researchers
can exploit full potential of this area. We hope to inspire further research and
application of IB and strategy theories in multiple bidder corporate acquisitions as such endeavors will be beneficial for both scholars and practitioners.

References

Acemoglu, D., Johnson, S., Robinson, J. & Thaicharoen, Y. 2003. Institutional cau-
　　ses, macroeconomic symptoms: Volatility, crises and growth. *Journal of Monetary
　　Economics*, 50(1): 49 – 123.

Acemoglu, D. & Johnson, S. 2003. *Unbundling Institutions*. National Bureau of Economic

Research. University of Chicago Press: 949 – 995.

Aguilera, R. V. & Dencker, J. C. 2011. Determinants of acquisition completion: A relational perspective.

Aguilera, R. V, Dencker, J. C. 2012. Determinants of acquisition completion.

Aktas, N. , De Bodt, E. & Roll, R. 2004. Market response to European regulation of business combinations. *Journal of Financial and Quantitative Analysis*, 39 (4): 731 – 757.

Amburgey, T. L. & Miner, A. S. 1992. Strategic momentum: The effects of repetitive, positional, and contextual momentum on merger activity. *Strategic Management Journal*, 13(5): 335 – 348.

Anand, B. N. & Khanna, T. 2000. The structure of licensing contracts. *The Journal of Industrial Economics*, 48(1): 103 – 135.

Anderson, J. E. & Marcouiller, D. 2002. Insecurity and the pattern of trade: An empirical investigation. *Review of Economics and Statistics*, 84(2): 342 – 352.

Andrade, G. , Mitchell, M. L. & Stafford, E. 2001. New evidence and perspectives on mergers.

Angwin, D. 2001. Mergers and acquisitions across European borders: National perspectives on preacquisition due diligence and the use of professional advisers. *Journal of World Business*, 36(1): 32 – 57.

Barkema, H. , Bell, J. & Pennings, J. M. E. 1996. Foreign entry, cultural barriers and learning. *Strategic Management Journal*, 17: 151 – 166.

Bazerman, M. H. & Samuelson, W. F. 1983. I won the auction but don't want the prize. *Journal of Conflict Resolution*, 27(4): 618 – 634.

Bebchuk, L. A. 1982. The case for facilitating competing tender offers. *Harvard Law Review*, 95(5): 1028 – 1056.

Beckman, C. M. & Haunschild, P. R. 2002. Network learning: The effects of partners' heterogeneity of experience on corporate acquisitions. *Administrative Science Quarterly*, 47(1): 92 – 124.

Berry, H. , Guillén, M. F. & Zhou, N. 2010. An institutional approach to cross – national distance. *Journal of International Business Studies*, 41(9): 1460 – 1480.

Bessler, W. , Schneck,C. & Zimmermann,J. 2015. Bidder contests in international mergers and acquisitions: The impact of toeholds, preemptive bidding, and termination fees. *International Review of Financial Analysis*. Online April 25.

Betton, S. & Eckbo, B. E. & Thorburn, K. S. 2009. Merger negotiations and the toehold puzzle. *Journal of Financial Economics*, 91(2): 158 – 178.

Betton, S. & Eckbo, B. E. 2000. Toeholds, bid jumps, and expected payoffs in takeovers. *Review of Financial Studies*, 13(4): 841 – 882.

Boone, A. L. & Mulherin, J. H. 2007. How are firms sold? *The Journal of Finance*, 62 (2): 847 – 875.

Bradley, M. , Desai, A. & Kim, E. H. 1988. Synergistic gains from corporate acquisitions and their division between the stockholders of target and acquiring firms. *Journal of Financial Economics*, 21(1): 3 –40.

Brandenburger, A. M. & Stuart, H. W. 1996. Value – based business strategy. *Journal of Economics & Management Strategy*, 5(1): 5 –24.

Brouthers, K. D. & Brouthers, L. E. 2000. Acquisition or Greenfield start – up? Institutional, cultural and transaction cost influences. *Strategic Management Journal*, 21(1): 89 –97.

Brouthers, K. D. 2002. Institutional, cultural and transaction cost influences on entry mode choice and performance. *Journal of International Business Studies*, 33(2): 203 –221.

Brouthers, K. D. 2013. A retrospective on: Institutional, cultural and transaction cost influences on entry mode choice and performance. *Journal of International Business Studies*, 44(1): 14 –22.

Buckley, P. J. & Casson, M. C. 1998. Analyzing foreign market entry strategies: Extending the internalization approach. *Journal of International Business Studies*, 29(3): 539 –561.

Bugeja, M. 2011. Foreign takeovers of Australian listed entities. *Australian Journal of Management*, 36(1): 89 – 107.

Bulow, J. & Klemperer, P. 1996. Auctions vs. negotiations. *American Economic Review*, 86(1): 180 –194.

Bulow, J. & Klemperer, P. 2009. Why do sellers (usually) prefer auctions? *The American Economic Review*, 99(4): 1544 – 1575.

Calori, R. , Lubatkin, M. & Very, P. 1994. Control mechanisms in cross – border acquisitions: An international comparison. *Organization Studies*, 15(3): 361 –379.

Capron, L. & Pistre, N. 2002. When do acquirers earn abnormal returns? *Strategic Management Journal*, 23(9): 781 –794.

Carline, N. F. , Linn, S. & Yadav, P. K. 2011. *Corporate Governance and Take Resistance*.

Chatterjee, P. 1986. *Nationalist Thought and the Colonial World: A Derivative Discourse*. Zed Books.

Chi, T. 1994. Trading in strategic resources: Necessary conditions, transaction cost problems, and choice of exchange structure. *Strategic Management Journal*, 15(4): 271 –290.

Chiles, T. H. & McMackin, J. F. 1996. Integrating variable risk preferences, trust, and transaction cost economics. *Academy of Management Review*, 21(1): 73 –99.

Ciobanu, R. , Brad, L. , Dobre, F. & Braşoveanu, I. V. 2014. Similarities between the acquirer and the target company in successful takeover bid offers. *Procedia Economics and Finance*, 15: 815 –821.

Coase, R. H. 1936. Book review (reviewing DH Macgregor, Industrial Combination (1935)). *Weltwirtschaftliches Archiv*, 44: 133.

Coase, R. H. 1937. The nature of the firm. *Economica*, 4(16): 386 – 405.

Collins, B. M. & Fabozzi, F. J. 1991. A methodology for measuring transaction costs. *Financial Analysts Journal*, 47(2): 27 – 36.

Cramton, P. & Schwartz A. 1991. Using auction theory to inform takeover regulation. *Journal of Law, Economics & Organization*, 7(1): 27 – 53.

Cramton, P. 1998. Ascending auctions. *European Economic Review*, 42(3): 745 – 756.

Crouch, C. 2005. *Capitalist Diversity and Change: Recombinant Governance and Institutional Entrepreneurs*. Oxford University Press.

Danbolt, J. & Maciver G. 2012. Cross – border versus domestic acquisitions and the impact on shareholder wealth. *Journal of Business Finance & Accounting*, 39(7 – 8): 1028 – 1067.

Dasgupta, S. & Hansen, R. 2008. *Auctions in Corporate Finance*. Handbook of Corporate Finance. Elsevier BV: 87 – 143.

Dasgupta, S. & Tsui, K. 2003. A "matching auction" for targets with heterogeneous bidders. *Journal of Financial Intermediation*, 12(4): 331 – 364.

Datta, D. K. & Puia, G. 1995. Cross – border acquisitions: An examination of the influence of relatedness and cultural fit on shareholder value creation in US acquiring firms. *MIR: Management International Review*, 35(4): 337 – 359.

Delios, A. & Henisz, W. I. 2000. Japanese firms' investment strategies in emerging economies. *Academy of Management Journal*, 43(3): 305 – 323.

Dikova, D. , Sahib, P. R. & Van, W. A. 2010. Cross-border acquisition abandonment and completion: The effect of institutional differences and organizational learning in the international business service industry, 1981 – 2001. *Journal of International Business Studies*, 41(2): 223 – 245.

Dragota, V. , Lipara, C. & Ciobanu, R. 2013. Agency problems and synergistic effects in romania: The determinants of the control premium*. *Finance a Uver*, 63(2): 197 – 219.

Eckbo, B. E. 1983. Horizontal mergers, collusion, and stockholder wealth. *Journal of Financial Economics*, 11(1): 241 – 273.

Erel, I. , Liao, R. C. & Weisbach, M. S. 2012. Determinants of cross – border mergers and acquisitions. *The Journal of Finance*, 67(3): 1045 – 1082.

Facci, M. & Masulis, R. W. 2005. The choice of payment method in European mergers and acquisitions. *The Journal of Finance*, 60(3): 1345 – 1388.

Gatignon, H. & Anderson, E. 1988. The multinational corporation's degree of control over foreign subsidiaries: An empirical test of a transaction cost explanation. *Journal of Law, Economics & Organization*, 4(2): 305 – 336.

Ghemawat, P. 2003. Semiglobalization and international business strategy. *Journal of In-*

ternational Business Studies, 34(2): 138 – 152.

Ghemawat, P. 2001. Distance still matters. *Harvard Business Review*, 79 (8): 137 – 147.

Gomes – Casseres, B. 1989. Joint ventures in the face of global competition. *MIT Sloan Management Review*, 30(3): 17.

Graebner, M. E. & Eisenhardt, K. M. 2004. The seller's side of the story: Acquisition as courtship and governance as syndicate in entrepreneurial firms. *Administrative Science Quarterly*, 49(3): 366 – 403.

Groner, M. , Groner, R. & Bischof, W. F. 1983. *Approaches to Heuristics: A Historical Review. Methods of Heuristics.* New Jersey: Lawrence Erlbaum Associates, Inc.

Guillén, M. 2005. *The Rise of Spanish Multinationals: European Business in the Global Economy.* Cambridge University Press.

Hall, P. A. & Soskice, D. 2001. An introduction to varieties of capitalism. *Varieties of capitalism: The institutional foundations of comparative advantage*, 1: 50 – 51.

Harzing, A. W. 2002. Acquisitions versus greenfield investments: International strategy and management of entry modes. *Strategic Management Journal*, 23(3): 211 – 227.

Haunschild, P. R. 1994. How much is that company worth? Interorganizational relationships, uncertainty, and acquisition premiums. *Administrative Science Quarterly*, 39 (3): 391 – 411.

Hedlund, G. , Rolander, D. , Bartlett, C. A. , Doz, Y. & Hedlund, G. 1990. *Action in Heterachies: New Approaches to Managing the MNC. Managing the Global Firm.* OX: Routledge.

Henisz, W. J. & Williamson, O. E. 1999. Comparative economic organization—within and between countries. *Business and Politics*, 1(3): 261 – 278.

Hil, C. W. 1990. Cooperation, opportunism, and the invisible hand: Implications for transaction cost theory. *Academy of Management Review*, 15(3): 500 – 513.

Hnatkovska, V. & Loayza. N. 2005. Volatility and Growth in J. Aizenman, Pinto, B. , eds. *Managing Economic Volatility and Crises: A Practitioner's Guide.* UK: Cambridge University Press.

Hofstede, G. 1980. *Culture's Consequences: Comparing Values, Behaviors, Institutions and Organizations Across Nations.* Thousand Oaks, California: Sage Publications, Inc.

Holl, P. & Kyriaziz, D. 1996. The determinants of outcome in UK take – over bids. *International Journal of the Economics of Business*, 3(2): 165 – 184.

Hope, O. K. , Thomas, W. & Vyas, D. 2011. The cost of pride: Why do firms from developing countries bid higher & quest. *Journal of International Business Studies*, 42 (1): 128 – 151.

Hotchkiss, E. S. , Qian, J. & Song, W. 2005. Holdups, renegotiation, and deal protection in mergers. *Available at SSRN 705365.*

Hueschen, G. W. 1951. Patents: Exclusive Licenses: Licensor and Licensee Relationship: Licensee's Obligations. *Michigan Law Review*, 49(5): 738 - 754.

Hunt, J. W. 1990. In takeovers and the consequences for (acquisition processes). *Strategic Management Journal*, 11(1): 69 - 77.

Hymer, S. 1960. On multinational corporations and foreign direct investment. *The Theory of Transnational Corporations*. London: Routledge for the United Nations.

Hymer, S. H. 1976. *The International Operations of National Firms: A Study of Direct Foreign Investment*. Cambridge, MA: MIT press: 139 - 155.

Ingram, P. & Clay, K. 2000. The choice - within - constraints new institutionalism and implications for sociology. *Annual Review of Sociology*, 26: 525 - 546.

Ionascu, D. , Meyer, K. E. & Estrin, S. 2004. Institutional distance and international business strategies in emerging economies.

Jackson, G. & Deeg, R. 2008. Comparing capitalisms: Understanding institutional diversity and its implications for international business. *Journal of International Business Studies*, 39(4): 540 - 561.

Jennings, R. H. & Mazzeo, M. A. 1991. Stock price movements around acquisition announcements and management's response. *Journal of Business*, 64(2): 139 - 163.

Jensen, M. C. & Ruback, R. S. 1983. The market for corporate control: The scientific evidence. *Journal of Financial Economics*, 11(1): 5 - 50.

Jensen, M. C. 1987. The free cash flow theory of takeovers: A financial perspective on mergers and acquisitions and the economy. In *Proceedings of a Conference sponsored by Federal Reserve Bank of Boston*: 102 - 143.

Johanson, J. & Vahlne, J. E. 1977. The internationalization process of the firm—A model of knowledge development and increasing foreign market commitments. *Journal of International Business Studies*, 8(1): 23 - 32.

Johanson, J. & Vahlne, J. E. 2009. The Uppsala internationalization process model revisited: From liability of foreignness to liability of outsidership. *Journal of International Business Studies*, 40(9): 1411 - 1431.

Kahneman, D. , Slovic, P. & Tversky, A. 1982. Judgment under uncertainty: Heuristics and biases. *Science*, 185(4157): 1124 - 1131.

Kahneman, D. , Diener, E. & Schwarz, N. 1999. *Well - being: Foundations of hedonic psychology*. Russell Sage Foundation.

Kahneman, D. & Frederick, S. 2002. Representativeness revisited: Attribute substitution in intuitive judgment. *Heuristics and Biases: The Psychology of Intuitive Judgment*: 1 - 30.

Kahneman, D. & Tversky, A. 1979. Prospect theory: An analysis of decision under risk. *Econometrica: Journal of the Econometric Society*, 47(2): 263 - 291.

Kahneman, D. 2003. Maps of bounded rationality: Psychology for behavioral economics. *The American Economic Review*, 93(5): 1449 - 1475.

Khanna, T. & Palepu, K. G. 2006. Emerging giants: Building world - class companies in developing countries. *Harvard Business Review*, 84(10): 60 - 69.

Kirzner, I M. 1986. *Subjectivism, Intelligibility and Economic Understanding: Essays in Honor of Ludwig M. Lachmann on His Eightieth Birthday*. Macmillan.

Kogut, B. & Zander, U. 1993. Knowledge of the firm and the evolutionary theory of the multinational corporation. *Journal of International Business Studies*, 24 (4): 625 - 645.

Kogut, B. & Singh, H. 1988. The effect of national culture on the choice of entry mode. *Journal of International Business Studies*, 19(3): 411 - 432.

Kogut, B. & Zander, U. 1992. Knowledge of the firm, combinative capabilities, and the replication of technology. *Organization Science*, 3(3): 383 - 397.

Kostova, T. , Roth, K. & Dacin, M. T. 2008. Institutional theory in the study of multinational corporations: A critique and new directions. *Academy of Management Review*, 33(4): 994 - 1006.

Kostova, T. & 1999. Transnational transfer of strategic organizational practices: A contextual perspective. *Academy of Management Review*, 24(2): 308 - 324.

Kostova, T. , Zaheer, S. 1999. Organizational legitimacy under conditions of complexity: The case of the multinational enterprise. *Academy of Management Review*, 24(1): 64 - 81.

Kristensen, P. H. & Zeitlin, J. 2005. Local players in global games. *The Strategic*.

La, P. R. , Lopez - de - Silanes, F. , Shleifer, A. & Vishny, R. W. 1997. Legal determinants of external finance. *Journal of Finance*, 52(3): 1131 - 1150.

La, P. R. , Lopez - de - Silanes, F. , Shleifer, A. & Vishny, R. 1998. Law and finance. *Journal of Political Economy*, 106(6): 1113 - 1155.

Laamanen, T. 2007. On the role of acquisition premium in acquisition research. *Strategic Management Journal*, 28(13): 1359 - 1369.

Laamanen, T. & Keil, T. 2008. Performance of serial acquirers: Toward an acquisition program perspective. *Strategic Management Journal*, 29(6): 663 - 672.

Larsson, R. & Finkelstein, S. 1999. Integrating strategic, organizational, and human resource perspectives on mergers and acquisitions: A case survey of synergy realization. *Organization Science*, 10(1): 1 - 26.

Lee, T. J. & Caves, R. E. 1998. Uncertain outcomes of foreign investment: Determinants of the dispersion of profits after large acquisitions. *Journal of International Business Studies*, 29(3): 563 - 581.

Lesmond, D. A, Ogden, J. P. & Trzcinka, C. A. 1999. A new estimate of transaction costs. *Review of Financial Studies*, 12(5): 1113 - 1141.

Levinthal, D. A. & Wu, B. 2010. Opportunity costs and non - scale free capabilities: Profit maximization, corporate scope, and profit margins. *Strategic Management Journal*, 31(7): 780 - 801.

Loayz, N. V., Ranciere, R., Servén, L. & Ventura, J. 2007. Macroeconomic volatility and welfare in developing countries: An introduction. *The World Bank Economic Review*, 21(3): 343 – 357.

Lucas, Jr R. E. 1978. Asset prices in an exchange economy. *Econometrica*, 46(6) 1429 – 1445.

Luo, Y. & Tung, R. L. 2007. International expansion of emerging market enterprises: A springboard perspective. *Journal of International Business Studies*, 38 (4): 481 – 498.

Madhok, A. 1996. Crossroads—the organization of economic activity: Transaction costs, firm capabilities, and the nature of governance. *Organization Science*, 7 (5): 577 – 590.

Madhok, A. 1997. Cost, value and foreign market entry mode: The transaction and the firm. *Strategic Management Journal*, 18(1): 39 – 61.

Maksimovic, V. & Phillips, G. 2002. Do conglomerate firms allocate resources inefficiently across industries? Theory and evidence. *Journal of Finance*, 57(2): 721 – 767.

March, J. G. 1991. Exploration and exploitation in organizational learning. *Organization Science*, 2(1): 71 – 87.

Markides, C. C., Ittner, C. D. 1994. Shareholder benefits from corporate international diversification: Evidence from US international acquisitions. *Journal of International Business Studies*, 25(2): 343 – 366.

Marshall, A. 1920. *Principles of Economics: An Introductory Volume.*

Mintzberg, H. 1973. Strategy – making in three modes. *California Management Review* (pre – 1986):44.

Mintzberg, H. 1973. *The Nature of Managerial Work.*

Moeller, S. B., Schlingemann, F. P. & Stulz, R. M. 2004. Firm size and the gains from acquisitions. *Journal of Financial Economics*, 73(2): 201 – 228.

Montgomery, C. & Singh, H. 1987. Corporate acquisition strategies and economic performance. *Strategic Management Journal*, 8(4): 377 – 386.

Morgan, G., Whitley, R. 2003. Introduction to special issue on the changing multinational firm. *Journal of Management Studies*, 40(3): 609 – 616.

Morosini, P., Shane, S. & Singh, H. 1998. National cultural distance and cross – border acquisition performance. *Journal of International Business Studies*, 29 (1): 137 – 158.

Myerson, R. B. 1981. Optimal auction design. *Mathematics of Operations Research*, 6 (1): 58 – 73.

Ning, L., Kuo, J. M., Strange, R. & Wang, B. 2014. International investors' reactions to cross – border acquisitions by emerging market multinationals. *International Business Review*, 23(4): 811 – 823.

Nisbett, R. E. & Ross, L. 1980. *Human Inference: Strategies and Shortcomings of Social*

Judgment.

North, D. C. 1990. A transaction cost theory of politics. *Journal of Theoretical Politics*, 2 (4): 355 – 367.

North, D. C. 1993. Institutions and credible commitment. *Journal of Institutional and Theoretical Economics (JITE)/Zeitschrift für die gesamte Staatswissenschaft*: 11 – 23.

Northcraft, G. B. & Neale, M. A. 1986. Opportunity costs and the framing of resource allocation decisions. *Organizational Behavior and Human Decision Processes*, 37(3): 348 – 356.

Officer, M. S. 2004. Collars and renegotiation in mergers and acquisitions. *The Journal of Finance*, 59(6): 2719 – 2743.

Parola, H. & Ellis, K. M. 2013. M&A negotiation stage: A review and future research directions. *Advances in Mergers & Acquisitions*, 12: 33 – 57.

Pasour, Jr E. C. 1991. The samaritan's dilemma and the welfare state. Policy, summer: 55 – 57.

Payne, J. W., Bettman, J. R. & Johnson, E. J. 1993. *The Adaptive Decision Maker.* Cambridge University Press.

Peng, M. W., Sun, S. L., Pinkham, B. & Chen, H. 2009. The institution – based view as a third leg for a strategy tripod. *The Academy of Management Perspectives*, 23 (3): 63 – 81.

Penrose, E. T. 1959. *The Theory of the Growth of the Firm.* Great Britain: Basil Blackwell and Mott Ltd.

Povel, P. & Singh, R. 2006. Takeover contests with asymmetric bidders. *Review of Financial Studies*, 19(4): 1399 – 1431.

Rappaport, A. 1979. Strategic analysis for more profitable acquisitions. *Harvard Business Review*, 57(4): 99 – 100.

Ravenscraft, D. J. & Scherer, F. M. 2011. *Mergers, Sell – offs, and Economic Efficiency.* Brookings Institution Press.

Reuer, J. J., Shenkar, O. & Ragozzino, R. 2004. Mitigating risk in international mergers and acquisitions: The role of contingent payouts. *Journal of International Business Studies*, 35: 19 – 32.

Robins, J. A. 1987. Organizational economics: Notes on the use of transaction – cost theory in the study of organizations. *Administrative Science Quarterly*, 32(1): 68 – 86.

Roll, R. 1986. The hubris hypothesis of corporate takeovers. *Journal of Business*, 59 (2): 197 – 216.

Salter, M. S. & Weinhold, W. A. 1978. Diversification via acquisition – creating value. *Harvard Business Review*, 56(4): 166 – 176.

Salter, M. S. & Weinhold, W. A. 1979. *Diversification through Acquisition: Strategies for Creating Economic Value.* Free Press.

Schwartz, A. 1988. The fairness of tender offer prices in utilitarian theory. *The Journal of*

Legal Studies, 17(1): 165 – 196.

Scott, W. R. 1995. *Institutions and Organizations*. Thousand Oaks, CA: Sage.

Serdar, D. I. & Erel, I. 2013. Economic nationalism in mergers and acquisitions. *The Journal of Finance*, 68(6): 2471 – 2514.

Shimizu, K. , Hitt, M. A. , Vaidyanath, D. & Pisano, V. 2004. Theoretical foundations of cross – border mergers and acquisitions: A review of current research and recommendations for the future. *Journal of International Management*, 10(3): 307 – 353.

Shleifer, A. & Vishny, R. W. 1992. Liquidation values and debt capacity: A market equilibrium approach. *The Journal of Finance*, 47(4): 1343 – 1366.

Simon, H. A. 1972. Theories of bounded rationality. *Decision and Organization*, 1(1): 161 – 176.

Stout, L. A. 1990. Are takeover premiums really premiums? Market price, fair value, and corporate law. *Yale Law Journal*, 99(6): 1235 – 1296.

Stulz, R. M. , Walkling, R. A. & Song, M. H. 1990. The distribution of target ownership and the division of gains in successful takeovers. *Journal of Finance*, 45(3): 817 – 833.

Tong, T. W. & Li, S. 2013. The assignment of call option rights between partners in international joint ventures. *Strategic Management Journal*, 34(10): 1232 – 1243.

Vaughn, K. I. 1980. Does it matter that costs are subjective? *Southern Economic Journal*, 46(3): 702 – 715.

Very, P. & Schweiger, D. M. 2001. The acquisition process as a learning process: Evidence from a study of critical problems and solutions in domestic and cross – border deals. *Journal of World Business*, 36(1): 11 – 31.

Wan, W. P. 2005. Country resource environments, firm capabilities, and corporate diversification strategies. *Journal of Management Studies*, 42(1): 161 – 182.

Weitzel, U. & Berns, S. 2006. Cross – border takeovers, corruption, and related aspects of governance. *Journal of International Business Studies*, 37(6): 786 – 806.

Werin, L. & Wijkander, H. 1992. *Contract economics*. Blackwell.

Whitley, R. , Morgan, G. , Kelly, W. & Sharpe, D. 2003. The changing Japanese multinational: Application, adaptation and learning in car manufacturing and financial services. *Journal of Management Studies*, 40(3): 643 – 672.

Williamson, O. E. 1973. Markets and hierarchies: Some elementary considerations. *The American Economic Review*, 63(2): 316 – 325.

Williamson, O. E. 1981. The economics of organization: The transaction cost approach. *American Journal of Sociology*, 87(3): 548 – 577.

Williamson, O. E. 1985. *The Economic Institutions of Capitalism*. Simon and Schuster.

Williamson, O. E. 1975. Markets and hierarchies. *New York*: 26 – 30.

Williamson, O. E. 1979. Transaction – cost economics: The governance of contractual relations. *Journal of Law and Economics*, 22(2): 233 – 261.

Witt, M. A. & Lewin, A. Y. 2007. Outward foreign direct investment as escape response to home country institutional constraints. *Journal of International Business Studies*, 38 (4): 579 - 594.

Zaheer, S. & Mosakowski E. 1997. The dynamics of the liability of foreignness: A global study of survival in financial services. *Strategic Management Journal*, 18(6): 439 - 463.

Zaheer, S. 1995. Overcoming the liability of foreignness. *Academy of Management Journal*, 38(2): 341 - 363.

Zajac, E. J. & Olsen C. P. 1993. From transaction cost to transactional value analysis: Implications for the study of interorganizational strategies. *Journal of Management Studies*, 30(1): 131 - 145.

Zhang, J. & He X. 2014. Economic nationalism and foreign acquisition completion: The case of China. *International Business Review*, 23(1): 212 - 227.

国际市场营销中细节文化差异应用研究

张若月[*]

【摘要】 经济全球化使得越来越多的国家和企业不断跻身于国际化的竞争中。也正因为如此,国家和地区间巨大的文化差异对商务活动的影响日渐明显。跨文化交际能力越强,企业越能迅速和顺畅地进入国外市场,规避风险,从而更容易取得国外消费群体的信任,获取更广阔的市场和更大的市场份额。而当今跨文化交际已不再是中国人见面握手、西方人拥抱和亲吻对方脸颊这么泛泛的区别。影响和决定企业成败的关键在于更深层次和更细节的文化差异对市场营销的影响。因此,为了获取成功,企业需要对文化有很强的敏感度,意识到文化的细节化差异。本文以产品及相关联的营销渠道管理为突破口来系统梳理市场营销中对文化差异的研究,提出尊重文化细节差异的基础上的市场营销策略。

【关键词】 跨文化交际、产品、网站、细节化差异

Application of Detailed Cultural Difference in International Marketing

Ruoyue Zhang[*]

Abstract With the development of globalization, more and more companies enter the global market. Just because of this, cross – cultural communication becomes more important than ever. A good understanding of how culture impacts the international business helps to manage risk better and identify the right business opportunities to seize, and generally becomes more easy to persuade foreign customers to strengthen the competition power to make the international business a success. Nowadays, cross – cultural communication does not only mean shaking hands for Chinese or kissing for Western people. What impacts the success of business is the detailed difference among different cultures. In order to be successful, companies should have

---

* 张若月,西安外国语大学商学院,讲师,研究方向:跨文化交际、消费文化。

strong cultural sensitivity and awareness of detailed cultural difference. This article aims to combine channel management to analyze the influence of detailed cultural difference on marketing to clarify the efficient marketing strategies based on the cross – cultural communication.

Key Words　Cross – Cultural Communication, Product, Website, Detailed Difference

1. 跨文化交际意识

　　商场中流行这样一句话,利益让世界越来越小,并逐渐变成了一个地球村,而地球村的形成并不意味着各国间文化差异的消失,相反,随着各国各企业间的贸易与合作变得越来越密切,文化的冲突也变得更常见,因此,国际商务的成功很大程度上依赖于国际营销技能对文化差异的掌控。因为一般在国际市场中,企业所面临的最激烈的竞争往往不是来自同行,而是来自文化差异导致的不同风俗习惯或信仰。

　　尤其进入 21 世纪以来,随着营销理论界对文化进行了持续和深入的研究,文化这一概念从纯粹作为营销的外生变量和研究的客体,变成了企业可以运用的营销手段。文化是一个社会中能够引导人们行为的价值、信仰和标准的总和。这些价值、信仰和标准形成了人们约定俗成的价值规范,决定这个社会中什么是对和错,什么是可接受和不可接受,什么是流行和不流行。文化环境看不见、摸不着,因此很容易被忽视,但却无时无刻不影响着人们的日常行为和价值观。近几年,管理和市场营销理论受文化的影响已逐渐成为学者的共识。越来越多的专家学者和业内人士认识到在商务环境中,文化差异往往成为跨国经营的无形壁垒。跨文化交际中因为文化差异而产生的不同行为标准在交流过程中造成误解的情况时有发生,有时会让人感觉比较尴尬,但又很难完全避免。然而合理的准备和训练有素的跨文化沟通技巧能有效地减少这种误解的产生,并在国际竞争中更自信、更有效地处理文化差异并避免尴尬,从而不断提高跨文化沟通的质量,以便帮助企业更好地规避风险,寻找机会,把握商机,并保证商业上的成功。因为对任何一家企业而言,良好的跨文化沟通意味着通畅、稳定的市场关系,而好的市场关系对企业则意味着快速增长的生产效率、更大的市场份额以及更多的利润。

　　正如很多经济学家曾指出的,好的跨文化沟通技巧依赖于我们有意识、有能力判断文化差异什么时候以及如何来影响商务交流,但在实际工作场合,能够完全将自己的文化放下而自如地与其他文化的人交流并不是一件很简单的事。

在营销活动中,文化差异最为敏感的因素是文化禁忌。例如,一位想打入中国市场的美国清洁剂制造商精心设计了这样一则广告:一群充满活力的中国人在兴高采烈地抛帽子,其中一顶绿色的帽子落到了一位男士头上。在广告设计中,公司本想通过"绿色"强调产品原料的天然与味道的清新,用来传递一个绿色健康的概念。同时在广告设计中也考虑到中国人的集体性,采用了"一群人"而非"一个人",可见公司在广告设计中煞费苦心,充分考虑了中西方文化存在的差异。然而公司却忽视了一个中国特有的现象:绿颜色的帽子对中国男士有一种特殊的含义,通常用绿帽子来指代妻子对丈夫的不忠。由此,该广告在中国市场的营销效果可想而知,而这样的企业在中国市场备受冷落也就变得理所当然了。

由此可见,文化差异随处可见,很难避免,但往往影响成败的并不是众所周知的文化差异,而是细节差异。忽视细节差异很容易导致貌似"周全"的市场战略全盘皆输。固然强烈的文化意识能够帮助我们更容易也更清楚地看到文化差异如何威胁商业的成功,而依赖于丰富的社会经验以及对沟通效果强烈的责任感的专业的跨文化意识可以帮助企业避免"因小失大"的噩梦。因此,在现代营销过程中,应该在细节上、在深层次上不断提高沟通技巧,否则产品技术再领先、品质再优良、价格再合理也无法占领市场。同时企业必须意识到文化差异中最为敏感的因素是文化禁忌。禁忌标志着一种文化与另一种文化差异的界限,触碰另一种文化的禁忌只会让该产品甚至该公司在目标国一败涂地。

2. 产品设计中的文化差异

众所周知,市场中最核心的因素是顾客,而顾客最关心的是产品,没有对产品设计的精心推敲,就谈不上在市场上的成功。在对产品进行分析时,文化差异的影响尤其重大,而这种差异性无形中增加了商务沟通的挑战性。向不同文化的消费者提供商品是一件具有挑战性的工作,因为各国家、各地区的文化价值观都不一样,所以消费者对产品的期望和需求差异很大。而这也增加了企业在不同文化市场完成工作的难度以及适应一种新的生活方式的难度。

要想进行准确的分析,企业必须在维护和实现自身企业目标的前提下尽量以该国家、该地区的文化价值立场去思考,充分考虑不同文化的消费者对商品的要求以及购买过程中影响决策的因素。也就是说,为了更好地了解和满足当地消费者,销售人员需要熟悉细节,从而准确掌握当地消费者的消费习惯和行为以及影响消费决策的因素,这样才有可能吸引当地消费者尝试自己公司的产品。即使是一个拥有国际营销经验的企业，要想设计出满足消费者需求的产品，也需要随时从细节上留意文化差异，从而保证该公司在国外市场拓展方面长期保持良好战绩，因为文化既是需求的传承也是需求的发展。例如营销学里的经典案例：联合利华在进入巴西时，因对当地文化进行了深刻、准确的分析而大获成功。除了对当地人在产品质量、味道等方面进行充分调研外，联合利华还注意到当地很多比较穷的人没有洗衣机，也有很多人在河里洗衣服，所以为了防止滑落水中，联合利华并没有沿用在欧美市场备受宠爱的纸质包装，而是设计了塑料包装；同时因为当地人收入低，对每周或每月的支出非常有计划性，因此对价格敏感，而且购买量不大，因此公司把当地的产品设计成小包装而不是欧美市场颇受喜爱的"家庭装"，以降低单次购买商品的成本，适应当地消费者的需求，从而大获成功。由此可见，要想将产品顺利推向国外市场，必须在细节上符合当地消费者的要求，切身考虑他们的喜好、需求甚至困难，这样才能真正被消费者接受，实现企业的拓展目标。

3. 网页设计中的文化差异

从营销战略上看，一个已经或想要跨国经营的公司应该意识到，在国外市场中考虑产品设计来迎合当地消费者对企业成功至关重要，但并不能完全实现企业拓展市场的目标。当今市场竞争激烈，在经济全球化发展的过程中，为了实现企业的战略目标，无论对于国际化程度较高的成熟市场还是刚被开发不久的新市场，企业都需要不断尝试新的营销手段来开拓市场。随着电子商务的不断发展，公司对网络的利用不断提高。虽不是所有的公司都通过网络进行营销，但在信息技术高速发展的今天，越来越多的企业意识到了网络的优势。好的网页设计的确能够更快更有效地帮助合作伙伴及消费者迅速、全面地了解企业信息。

因此，在考虑产品设计的同时，企业也应关注各国网站的设计，如网页颜色的选择、导读条位置的设计、动画的制作甚至声音的选择。只有这样，才能与客户畅通交流，并与他们的期望和价值观保持同步，从而有效开拓市场。网页直接传递公司想要与目标客户交流的信息、交流的方式以及交流的可能。当国外目标消费者想要通过网站了解公司及其产品时，公司需要根据当地文化调整网站内容以适应当地消费者的需求。但当今市场，网页已不再是关于公司和产品的文字的简单排列，而是文本、图形、声音和动画资源的集合。既能体现企业文化又迎合当地消费者需求的网页设计可以帮助企业大量获得消费者的反馈信息，帮助企业做出正确的决策,从而更好地了解和进入目标市场。

　　根据文化差异调整得越多,对目标市场的适应越好,企业在国际商务中成功的可能性就越大。例如,高语境文化善于运用非语言手段传递信息表达情感,因此比较喜欢用动画效果,倾向于用 Flash 等工具来表现主旨和传递网页内容。而低语境文化国家使用动画则是为了强调动态链接和公司标志,如麦当劳,其在中文网站运用大量彩色图片和动态Flash 介绍新产品或公司的新动向,而在欧美地区其网站简单、静态,只有几个简单的链接来展示公司的新产品。不同文化有不同的价值观和生活观,麦当劳在瑞士的网页广告里表现了一个男士独自悠闲地享受音乐,生动地展示了低语境国家人所追求的悠闲生活状态——在独处中找到自我,享受生活。而在中国,都是以家庭、朋友的欢聚来展现幸福生活的状态,于是麦当劳的广告则更多以欢聚为主题。同时,低语境国家网页设计比较直观,人们能够轻松、容易地找到自己感兴趣的信息。而在高语境国家,网页世界的隐藏度较高,很多信息被隐藏在大的标题里,只有将鼠标放在该标题上,才会显示包含的信息模块。因此,浏览者必须花较多的时间才能找到自己想要的信息。这种细节的考虑让不同文化的人在浏览网站时都能很顺畅地找到自己想了解的信息。

4. 网络语言中的文化差异

　　语言的差异直接影响广告的理解和信息的接收程度,而语言直接受社会文化的影响和制约,并反映当时的社会文化。一般而言,为了适应目标市场,让目标消费者以及合作伙伴能快速便捷地获取企业级产品的相关信息,企业都会升级不同语言的网站。而将公司网站翻译成各种目标语言之前,企业最好先完善英语网站,因为英语是受众面最广的交流方式。从某种程度上来讲,英语是一种国际语言,是国际交流中最常见的语言之一,英语网站最容易被更多的消费者理解和接受。但在翻译及表达时应尽量避免语义误解。例如,tambo 这个单词在玻利维亚、哥伦比亚等国指路边店,在阿根廷、乌拉圭等国指奶牛场,但是在智利却指妓院。而 tomorrow 在英语国家就是指当天午夜 12 点到第二天午夜 12 点,是指一段非常具体的时间,而在西班牙语国家,tomorrow 并不是这么具体的时间概念,而是指将来的任意时间。因此在网页设计中,一定要保证语言在目标文化中准确传递企业想要表达的意思。

　　另外,在翻译的过程中应注意语言文化的社会性。丰富的跨文化意识体现在了解一个词汇在不同的语言文化里会有不同的意思,以及对于目标语言客户熟悉和习惯的语言表达方式,从而达到营销目的。例如,耐克那句耳熟能详的广告语"Just do it",一开始翻译成中文"想做就做",广告播出没多久,就在当地引起轩然大波,家长们纷纷投诉,认为这句话会误导青少年做事不计后果,不负责任。后来把它改成"该做就做",才平息这场风波。因为西方的教育崇尚自我和追求个性张扬,而中国文化则一直强调内敛。由此可见,企业在传递公司理念的同时应尽可能了解和适应当地受众群体的文化特点。

5. 广告设计中的文化差异

除了网页外,广告也是当今市场上最常见的与顾客沟通的方式之一。越来越多的消费者习惯从各种广告中获取产品信息。在这种市场沟通中,企业是否考虑到文化的差异,尤其是细节文化,会直接影响广告效果。其中,风俗习惯的差异对广告的影响最为明显:在广告创作中,如果不注意所在地区的风俗习惯,就会引发笑话甚至惹怒当地人民,也就达不到广告的效果。曾经有一种知名品牌饮料的广告画在西方各国取得了巨大成功,但是在阿拉伯世界却惨遭败绩。这幅广告是由从左到右的四个画面构成的:第一个画面是炎炎烈日下干渴难耐的男子形象;第二个画面是这个男子畅饮该品牌饮料的情景;第三个画面是该品牌产品的特写;第四个画面是喝完饮料后满脸惬意的男子形象。但是,阿拉伯人的阅读习惯是从右到左读,所以在阿拉伯人看来,广告中的饮料正是造成那个男子干渴难耐的原因。因此,这则广告的效果可想而知。

同时,广告设计中也应考虑当地消费者的生活习惯。生活习惯看不见、摸不着,但却无处不在,并直接影响消费者的购买力。力士香皂在德国的广告片中是一位明星手拿力士香皂淋浴的镜头,而英国的力士香皂广告片中,那位淋浴的明星却改为在浴缸里为力士做广告。这个小小的差别其实反映了德国人偏爱淋浴,英国人则偏爱池浴的不同生活习惯。这个广告因为细节的考虑让消费者产生一种熟悉感,从而刺激了购买的欲望。由此可见,在广告设计中,创意固然重要,但无论什么样的创意都应建立在从细节上了解和尊重当地习俗。尊重风俗文化也就是尊重当地人,这会让当地消费者对产品以及公司产生一种亲近感,当然也就能更好地实现营销目的。

6. 结束语

文化既可以是一个民族不断积淀的个性性格的传承,也可以是新经济下的时尚创新。它是一个民族、一个地区特有的价值观和评判标准。

随着经济全球化以及经济强国不断的市场扩张,商业中的跨文化交际已经成为不可避免的话题。缺少跨文化沟通意识,不理解文化的变化,或者忽视不同文化之间的差异,都会大大影响企业的竞争优势。只有具备良好的跨文化意识,提高对文化差异的敏感度,充分意识到并不断熟悉文化差异的细微之处,才能不断提高自己的跨文化沟通意识和技巧。无论是产品设计还是营销战略的设计,都应根据市场的不同需求而采取差异化设计。不管到了哪个国家或地区,都应将自己定位为当地的公司、当地的人,缩小与消费者的距离,破除唯我独尊的心态,用心体会文化的细节差异,这样企业才能在激烈的竞争中击败对手,在市场中立于不败之地。

参 考 文 献

Würtz,E. 2006. Intercultural communication on web sites:A cross – cultural analysis of web sites from high – context cultures and low – context cultures. *Journal of Computer – Mediated Communication*,11:274 – 299.

Beamer,L. 2003. *Intercultural Communication in the Global Workplace*. Tsinghua University Press:5 – 10.

杰伊·巴尼. 2010. 战略管理. 机械工业出版社:23 – 35.

李峥. 2008. 从文化差异视角看外来商品广告的中国化. 科技资讯,(6):220 – 223.

苗新宇. 2008. 商品营销广告与文化. 商场现代化,(1):125.

王春媚. 2005. 广告的文化内涵研究. 河海大学硕士学位论文:15 – 23.

王春媚,万亦农,张雷. 2006. 中西方的文化差异与广告理解. 商业经济,(2):120 – 121.

吴兆春. 2011. 市场营销中"文化"的研究综述. 商业时代,(9):34 – 35.

张锐. 2011. 品牌国际化营销的 N 条路径. 中外企业文化,(2):5 – 9.

收入差距对国民幸福感影响的实证研究
——基于文化的调节作用

许芳　黄卫*

【摘要】 本文利用基尼系数、国民幸福指数和 Hofstede 国家文化模型分析收入差距对国民幸福感的影响,发现收入差距和国民幸福感负向相关。文化对收入差距和国民幸福感之间的关系有重要的调节作用,其中权力距离、不确定规避对收入差距和国民幸福感之间的关系有正向调节作用,集体主义对收入差距和国民幸福感之间的关系有负向调节作用。另外,从文化引导方面对中国国民幸福感的提升提出了相关建议。

【关键词】 收入差距、国民幸福感、国家文化

An Empirical Study on the Impact of Income Gap on People's Sense of Happiness— Based on Adjustment of Culture

Fang Xu　Wei Huang

Abstract　This paper uses the Gini coefficient, the people happiness index and Hofstede cultural dimensions model to analyze the effect of income disparity on people's sense of happiness. It was found that the income gap and people happiness correlate negatively. Culture plays an important regulatory role on the relationship of income disparity and happiness. Power distance and uncertainty avoidance have a positive regulation effect on the relationship of income disparity and happiness, but collectivism has a negative regulation effect on the relationship of income disparity and happiness. This paper also puts forward some relevant suggestions about the promotion of China's national happiness from the aspect of culture.

Key Words　Income Gap, People's Sense of Happiness, National Culture

* 许芳,南京师范大学商学院教授、研究生导师,研究方向:跨文化研究、人力资源管理和组织生态学;黄卫,南京师范大学商学院企业管理研究生,研究方向:企业文化、跨文化研究。

1. 引言

幸福超越国界,但各国幸福程度却千差万别。幸福指数可以衡量一个国家的国民幸福感,在监控国家整体运行态势的基础上又能够反映民众满意程度。联合国发布的《2015年世界幸福报告》显示,瑞士是世界上最快乐的国家,其次是冰岛、丹麦、挪威和加拿大。而中国在2015年的国民幸福感排名中列第84位。可见,中国人的幸福感在世界范围内处于中下水平。

近年来中国发展速度让世人瞩目,然而经济的大幅增长并未促使国民幸福水平同步提升。各种现实表明,大部分中国民众正在为教育、住房和医疗所累,GDP的高速增长并没有给人们带来更高的幸福感。相反,中国经济繁荣创造的财富未能在国民间均等地分配,贫富差距的拉大正在吞噬中产阶级,并使得越来越多的家庭可能因一次大病而陷入衰落,这会导致我国社会根基的不稳定,并掣肘中国经济可持续发展。"不患寡而患不均",人们天生对公平有着强烈的执着。大量研究发现,社会上的不平等现象,特别是收入差距与国民幸福感有很大的相关性(何立新和潘春阳,2011)。

然而,收入差距对世界各国的影响不尽相同,收入差距的大小与幸福感的高低并不完全匹配。如美国基尼系数为0.408,属于收入差距较大的国家,但其幸福感指数达到7.08,在世界排名中居第15位。而摩洛哥基尼系数为0.395,和美国大致相似,但其幸福指数为4.88,在世界平均水平之下。近10年来,大量跨文化学者开始研究文化与国民幸福感(陆洛,2007)。Markus和Kitayama(2006)提出了文化常模模型(Culturol Norm Model),其基本假设是:"合乎规范的行为被认为是'好的'或'对的'。"也就是说,个体按照社会规范行事的程度决定着他们的生活满意度,该模型从理论和实证两个层面表明文化对于幸福感具有决定性影响。因此,我们可以认为在收入差距对国民幸福感产生影响的过程中,文化起着很大的调节作用。

以往研究大多只关注绝对收入和相对收入与幸福感之间的关系,对收入差距与幸福感的关系的研究相对较少,并且忽略了文化方面的因素,因而遭到一些跨文化学者的抨击。事实上,幸福感存在非常重要的跨国差异,特别是东西方文化差异。本文在关注收入差距与国家幸福感的关系时,加入文化这个调节变量,在全球范围内进行跨文化分析。

2. 理论分析与假设

2.1　收入差距与国民幸福感

现实中大多数人持有物质幸福感,认为高收入、高享受可以得到更高的幸福感(袁正、郑欢和韩骁,2013)。Easterlin(1995)认为,主观幸福感随自身收入的提高正向变化,随他人收入的提高反向变化。Luttmer(2004)发现,当邻居收入水平提升时,人们会感觉不幸福。可见,既然相对收入影响人们的幸福感水平,那么收入差距也会影响国民幸福感。

人们对于不平等的反应不同。当人们发现身边其他人的经济情况变好时,会对自身有一个乐观预期,人们的幸福感会提高,这就是"正向隧道效应"。但如果经济增长成果只惠及小部分人,大部分人被隔离于经济繁荣成果之外,以至于收入差距过大,低收入者没有得到预期结果,则此时"负向隧道效应"将展现出来,人们会变得不满和愤怒,幸福感水平将降低。"相对剥夺理论"是指当人们将自身与其他参照物进行比较时发现自身处于劣势状态下所产生的负面心理体验,人们此时会有强烈的不公平感并导致幸福感降低。

Morawetz(1997)最早对这个问题进行研究,发现收入分配较为公平的村庄平均幸福感水平显著高于收入差距较大的村庄。Hagerty(2000)利用多个国家 25 年的数据证实,收入分配差距越大的国家,其民众的平均幸福感越低。Schwarze 和 Harpfer(2007)也发现,德国基尼系数与居民生活满意度之间显著负相关。Graham 和 Felton(2004)、Alesina(2006)、Oshio 和 Kobayashi(2011)通过对拉美国家、欧洲国家、美国和日本进行研究得出类似的结论。Brockman 等(2009)利用世界价值观数据进行研究,发现收入差距扩大及其带来的相对剥夺感导致了我国平均幸福感水平的降低。这些以往研究证实,当收入差距扩大时,"负向隧道效应"和"相对剥夺感"占据主导地位。因此本文提出以下假设:

*H*1:收入差距与国民幸福感负相关。

2.2　文化的调节作用

以往跨文化研究证实了不同国家的生活满意程度呈现较为稳定的差异性。文化对国民幸福感有重要影响(Dezhu Ye , Yew – Kwang Ng & Yujun Lian, 2014)。收入差距对幸福感的影响在于社会能够承受收入不平等的程度,在此过程中文化因素起很大作用。因此,我们可以认为文化对收入差距和幸福感的关系产生重要的调节作用。Hofstede 国家文化维度模型的五个不同维度分别是权力距离、集体主义—个人主义、阴柔气质—阳刚气质、不确定性规避和长期导向—短期导向。本文将仔细区分不同国家文化在这五个维度上的异同,并且探究其对收入差距与幸福感关系的调节作用。

权力距离是人们对于社会权力分配不平等的接纳和容忍程度,即人们在多大程度上视其为正常现象。Hofstede 认为权力距离越大,越可能导致不平等。收入分配平等程度和权力距离正相关,权力距离越大,社会收入差距会越大,并且幸福感水平和国家权力距离间明显负相关。Arrindell 等(1997)发现权力距离与国民幸福感是负相关关系(1997)。

根据以往大量的幸福感跨文化研究可得出结论:个人主义国家比集体主义国家有更强的幸福感感受(王淑燕和奚彦辉,2008)。在集体主义文化中,个人服从于集体,个体利益让步于集体利益,强调社会秩序的和谐统一。个人主义文化则强调自我支配和控制,主张个人利益,个体有较大的自主选择权,不容易受集体束缚。不同文化的国家拥有不同的社会特征,成员的自由平等程度与自我选择的实现程度也存在较大差别。在实证方面,Arrindell 等(1997)证实了个人主义和主观幸福感显著正相关。

Barnett 和 Baruch 等(2003)进行了大量研究,发现在阴柔气质得分较高的国家,女性往往有更多的社会角色和选择权利、较高的健康水平自我评价、较低的疾病发生率,从而产生更高水平的幸福感。高阴柔气质社会给女性更多的空间来选择自己的生活,并且能够提高全社会的平均幸福水平。Diener、Rechner 和 Arrindell(1997)也认为阳刚气质国家的特点是社会竞争意识强烈、较大的工作压力和较低的工作满意度,相比而言,阴柔气质国家有明显偏高的平均幸福感得分。

根据 Hofstede 的国家文化维度数据和 Arrindell(1997)的研究发现,不确定性规避与主观幸福感负相关。高不确定规避国家的民众对各种不确定性事件较为担忧,并设法避免,通常伴随着紧张和压力。从世界民族层面来看,有的民族把生活中各种未知和不确定情况视为大敌,也有民族对同样的情况坦然视之,这就直观地体现了不同民族文化在对待不确定性情况上有很大不同,并直接导致各国不确定性规避数值的高低不同。

长期导向的社会重视潜在的利益和结果。凡事考虑未来,愿意为目标不断奉献,牺牲现有的满足感。长期导向可以减少未来的不确定性,并且提供一个基础的满足感。短期导向的社会重视现在的利益和结果,注重当前的生活和享受,不愿意为将来牺牲现在,家庭生活比较宽容。Chui 和 Kwok(2008)指出,高度短期导向国家的居民在自己有需求时会较少帮助别人,居民在遭遇困难时产生无助感,这会减少人们的幸福感。短期导向的社会注重竞争,社会比较通常产生一个胜利者和许多失败者,会使社会平均的主观幸福感降低。

基于以上分析,本文提出以下假设:

H 2a:权力距离对收入差距与国民幸福感的关系有正向调节作用。

H 2b:个人主义和集体主义对收入差距与国民幸福感的关系有负向调节作用。

H 2c:阴柔气质和阳刚气质对收入差距与国民幸福感的关系有正向调节作用。

H 2d:不确定性规避对收入差距与国民幸福感的关系有正向调节作用。

H 2e:长期导向和短期导向对收入差距与国民幸福感的关系有负向调节作用。

3.　数据与变量

本文的因变量是幸福指数(GDH),用以衡量国家整体幸福感水平,数据来自联合国可持续发展解决方案网络(SDSN)制作并发布的《2015年全球幸福指数报告》(The World Happiness Report 2015)。本文的自变量是基尼系数(GINI),用以衡量国家收入差距和社会财富分配平等程度。所使用数据来自联合国大学经济发展研究院编制的世界各国收入公平性调查数据。本文的调节变量是国家文化,具体来自 Hofstede 国家文化模型的五个维度,分别是权力距离(PDI)、个人主义和集体主义(IDV)、阴柔气质和阳刚气质(MAS)、不确定性规避(UAI)、长期导向和短期导向(TOWVS)。本文采用 Hofstede 国家文化五维度模型,关于各个维度的具体数据来自 Hofstede 文化中心的调查研究。

由于幸福指数、基尼系数和国家文化各维度的数据在整合后所涉及的国家存在不一致及有些数据存在缺失,最终经过分析汇总,共选取了全球 51 个国家的样本作为研究对象。

4.　数据分析及结果

4.1　描述性分析结果

从表 1 的描述性分析结果可以看出,幸福指数、基尼系数和国家文化各维度的均值和标准差及各变量之间的相关系数。基尼系数与幸福指数显著相关,可知收入差距与国民幸福感之间显著相关。国家文化各维度中的权力距离、集体主义和个体主义与幸福指数存在显著相关关系,而阳刚气质和阴柔气质、不确定性规避、长期导向和短期导向与幸福指数不显著相关。接下来,本文将对幸福指数、基尼系数和国家文化各维度进行回归分析,进一步验证收入差距与国民幸福感的相关关系以及国家文化各维度对其关系的调节作用。

表 1 变量的均值、标准差和相关系数

变量	均值	标准差	GDH	GINI	PDI	IDV	MAS	UAI	TOWVS
GDH	6.072	0.092	1						
GINI	0.350	0.076	-0.553***	1					
PDI	57.78	21.43	-0.660**	-0.528***	1				
IDV	46.14	23.47	-0.591***	-0.640***	-0.614***	1			
MAS	47.69	20.89	-0.060	0.081	0.200	-0.019	1		
UAI	65.71	22.73	-0.226	-0.003	0.222	-0.240	0.001	1	
TOWVS	51.58	23.38	-0.025	-0.273	0.056	0.068	-0.076	0.053	1

注:P < 0.1;* p < 0.05;** p < 0.01;*** p < 0.001。

4.2 回归分析与回归结果

本文采用分层回归验证权力距离对收入差距与国民幸福感之间关系的影响,首先在模型 1 中进行基尼系数、权力距离与幸福指数的回归,其次在模型 2 中加入基尼系数与权力距离的交互项,进行基尼系数、权力距离和该交互项对国民幸福指数的回归。如表 2 所示,基尼系数与幸福指数显著负相关,因此收入差距与幸福感之间存在显著的负相关关系,由此 *H*1 得以证明。基尼系数与权力距离的交互项系数显著为正,说明权力距离对收入差距与幸福感的关系有正向调节作用,由此 *H*2*a* 得到证明。

表 2 权力距离对收入差距与国民幸福感调节作用的层次回归结果

自变量	模型 1	模型 2
基尼系数	-3.418*	-4.501**
权力距离	-0.022***	-0.017**
交互项		
基尼系数×权力距离		0.216*
调整 R^2	0.472	
Δ 调整 R^2		0.042*
F 值	23.336	18.048

注:P < 0.1;* p < 0.05;** p < 0.01;*** p < 0.001。

　　采用分层回归验证集体主义对收入差距与国民幸福感之间关系的影响,首先在模型 1 中进行基尼系数、集体主义与幸福指数的回归,其次在模型 2 中加入基尼系数与集体主义的交互项,进行基尼系数、集体主义和该交互项对国民幸福指数的回归。如表 3 所示,基尼系数与集体主义的交互项系数显著为负,说明集体主义对收入差距与幸福感的关系有负向调节作用。因此,$H2b$ 得到证明。

表 3　集体主义对收入差距与国民幸福感调节作用的层次回归结果

自变量	模型 1	模型 2
基尼系数	-3.565^{*}	8.108^{**}
集体主义	0.016^{**}	0.124^{***}
交互项		
基尼系数×集体主义		-0.333^{***}
调整 R^2	0.376	
Δ 调整 R^2		0.210^{***}
F 值	16.052	25.268

注:$P<0.1$;$*p<0.05$;$**p<0.01$;$***p<0.001$。

　　采用分层回归验证阳刚气质对收入差距与国民幸福感之间关系的影响,首先在模型 1 中进行基尼系数、阳刚气质与幸福指数的回归,其次在模型 2 中加入基尼系数与阳刚气质的交互项,进行基尼系数、阳刚气质和该交互项对国民幸福指数的回归。如表 4 所示,基尼系数与阳刚气质的交互项系数不显著,说明阳刚气质对收入差距与幸福感关系的正向调节作用不显著。因此,$H2c$ 没有得到证明。

表 4　阳刚气质对收入差距与国民幸福感调节作用的层次回归结果

自变量	模型 1	模型 2
基尼系数	-6.653^{***}	-12.987^{**}
阳刚气质	-0.001	-0.039
交互项		
基尼系数×阳刚气质		0.130
调整 R^2	0.277	
Δ 调整 R^2		0.031
F 值	10.558	7.935

注:$P<0.1$;$*p<0.05$;$**p<0.01$;$***p<0.001$。

　　采用分层回归验证不确定性规避对收入差距与国民幸福感之间关系的影响,首先在模型 1 中进行基尼系数、不确定性规避与幸福指数的回归,其次在模型 2 中加入基尼系数与不确定性规避的交互项,进行基尼系数、不确定性规避和该交互项对国民幸福指数的回归。如表 5 所示,基尼系数与不确定性规避的交互项系数显著为正,说明不确定性规避对收入差距与幸福感的关系有正向调节作用。因此,$H2d$ 得到证明。

表5　不确定性规避对收入差距与国民幸福感调节作用的层次回归结果

自变量	模型 1	模型 2
基尼系数	－ 6. 675***	－ 14. 469***
不确定性规避	－ 0. 009	－ 0. 057**
交互项		
基尼系数 × 不确定性规避		0. 134*
调整 R^2	0. 330	
Δ 调整 R^2		0. 068
F 值	13. 317	11. 565

注: $P < 0.1$; $*p < 0.05$; $**p < 0.01$; $***p < 0.001$。

　　用分层回归验证长期导向对收入差距与国民幸福感之间关系的影响,首先在模型 1 中进行基尼系数、长期导向与幸福指数的回归,其次在模型 2 中加入基尼系数与长期导向的交互项,进行基尼系数、长期导向和该交互项对国民幸福指数的回归。如表 6 所示,基尼系数与长期导向的交互项系数不显著,说明长期导向对收入差距与幸福感关系的正向调节作用不显著。因此,$H2e$ 没有得到证明。

表6　长期导向对收入差距与国民幸福感调节作用的层次回归结果

自变量	模型 1	模型 2
基尼系数	7. 290***	－ 5. 837
长期导向	－ 0. 007	0. 004
交互项		
基尼系数 × 长期导向		－ 0. 031
调整 R^2	0. 311	
Δ 调整 R^2		0. 003
F 值	12. 280	8. 119

注: $P < 0.1$; $*p < 0.05$; $**p < 0.01$; $***p < 0.001$。

5.　实证结果分析

本文基于全球 51 个国家的数据样本，以文化作为调节变量对收入差距与幸福感的关系进行了研究，通过分层逐次回归，最终得出收入差距与国民幸福感负相关。国家文化维度模型里的权力距离与不确定性规避对收入差距与幸福感的关系有显著的正向调节作用，而集体主义对收入差距与幸福感的关系有显著的负向调节作用。其关系如下：

5.1　权力距离对收入差距与国民幸福感的调节作用

根据以往学者的研究成果和本文的研究发现，收入差距与国民幸福感之间负相关，即收入差距越大，国民幸福感越低。经过分层回归，本文证实权力距离对收入差距与国民幸福感的关系有正向调节作用。所以权力距离越大，收入差距与国民幸福感的负相关程度越高。权力距离被界定为组织成员对于权力分配不平等的期待和接纳程度。高权力距离国家的特征是认可权力和等级的不平等，等级顺序严格，掌权者享有特权，不同权力地位的人难以平等相处。而低权力距离的社会认为每个人都有平等的权利，认为掌权者没有特权，权力的使用应该合法化，处于不同权力地位的人应相互信任。较大的权力距离会造成社会不同等级阶层的分化，加剧中下阶层民众的不公平感和对收入差距的强烈感受，使其幸福感程度下降，并拉低国家平均幸福感得分。因此，权力距离对收入差距和国民幸福感的关系产生正向调节作用。

5.2　个人主义和集体主义对收入差距与国民幸福感的调节作用

经过回归分析，本文发现集体主义对收入差距与国民幸福感的关系有负向调节作用。即国家的集体主义水平越高，收入差距与国民幸福感的负相关程度越高；个人主义水平越高，收入差距与国民幸福感的负相关程度越低。各个国家之间的个人主义水平有明显差异。一个国家的个人主义水平越高，其公民对自由的偏好就会越强烈。自由是个人主义者的理想，而平等则是集体主义者的愿望。因此，当收入差距出现时，个人主义的国家居民崇尚自由和个性，个人自由意识优于平等意识，会认可收入差距的存在，对收入差距并不会产生较大的反应。集体主义国家的居民认为平等意识高于自由意识，认为和谐一致是社会的终极目标，厌恶各种差异，反对社会上存在的不平等现象，收入差距越大，民众的幸福感越低。因此，集体主义对收入差距与国民幸福感的关系产生负向调节作用。

5.3 阴柔气质和阳刚气质对收入差距与国民幸福感的调节作用

本文通过实证分析发现,阳刚气质对收入差距与幸福感关系的调节作用不显著。阴柔气质国家的民众注重人际关系和生活质量,重视女性权利,女性有较好的社会地位和更多的机会,能够自由地进行自我选择,人们偏好平等和宽容,政府注重环境保护和改善生活环境。根据以往的调查研究,女性往往比男性有更高程度的幸福感水平。阳刚气质国家更注重挑战、提升和收入,强调男性权威,以公平进行奖励,政府以牺牲生活环境换取经济增长。Hofstede证实阳刚气质和阴柔气质对幸福感有影响,它们之间是负相关关系。但是两种维度的国家民众在对公平的偏好以及对收入差距的反应上并无较大区别,所以阴柔气质和阳刚气质对收入差距与幸福感之间的关系不产生影响。

5.4 不确定性规避对收入差距与国民幸福感的关系有正向调节作用

对于所有国家,幸福和不确定规避都是负相关关系。本次研究发现,不确定性规避对收入差距与幸福感的关系有正向调节作用,即不确定性规避程度越高,收入差距与幸福感之间的负相关程度越高。强不确定性规避国家的居民认为生活中的不确定性是一种持续性的威胁,必须与之抗争,人们压力较大,害怕模糊的情况和不常见的风险,认为差异是危险的,对健康和金钱担心较多,把成功或失败归结为环境或者运气。在强不确定性规避的国家,人们会厌恶收入差异,担心收入差距带来的财政危机,进而幸福感降低。弱不确定性规避国家的居民认为不确定性是生活的常态,有较少的压力和焦虑,较少担心健康和金钱,认为成功或失败取决于个人的能力,敢于冒险,有较强的成就动机,对工作条件乐观,较少情绪化。在弱不确定性规避的国家,人们对收入差距不会有较大的担忧,主观幸福感水平高。因此,不确定性规避对收入差距与幸福感的关系有正向调节作用。

5.5 长期导向和短期导向对收入差距与国民幸福感关系的调节作用

本文通过实证分析最终证实,长期导向对收入分配与幸福感关系的调节作用不显著。长期导向的社会注重面向未来的回报、务实的美德,尤其是节俭、持久性,并适应不断变化的情况,重视潜在的利益和结果,凡事考虑未来,愿意为目标不断奉献,牺牲现有的满足感,家庭成员之间比较谦让。长期导向可以减少未来的不确定性,并且提供一个基础的满足感。短期导向的社会重视现在的利益和结果,注重当前的生活和享受,不愿意为将来牺牲现在,家庭生活比较宽容,没有过多的长幼次序。在长期导向的国家,人们有长远的打算和长期较高的幸福感。在短期导向的国家,人们更加注重消费,注重当前的享受,也可以得到较高的物质幸福感。在以往的研究中,长期导向和短期导向与幸福感是负相关关系,经本文验证,长期导向和短期导向对收入差距与幸福感的调节作用不显著。

6. 结论与建议

本文从跨文化角度分析了不同文化维度对收入差距与国民幸福感之间关系的影响。首先,通过实证分析验证了之前大量研究得出的收入差距与国民幸福感负相关的结论。因此,降低收入差距可以减少人们的不公平感和其他负面情绪,并有效提升国民幸福感。其次,文化具有非常丰富的内涵,作为一种无形的工具和潜移默化的力量,它对收入差距和国民幸福感有重要的调节作用,其中权力距离、不确定性规避维度对收入差距和幸福感产生正向调节作用,个人主义和集体主义维度对收入差距和幸福感的关系为负向调节。所以,对国家文化某些方面进行改进也是全面提升国民幸福感水平的途径。

21世纪的中国正经历着经济快速发展与产业转型的关键时期,对于中国国民幸福感水平的提升,本文提出以下建议:

(1)政府必须关注国家收入分配制度公平与否,建立符合我国发展现状并有效保障公平的收入分配制度和秩序,在努力扭转城乡、区域、行业和社会成员之间收入差距不断扩大的趋势的同时,关注低收入者的利益保障,让经济发展成果惠及更多低收入层次民众,缩小我国贫富差距,并且减少收入不平等给民众幸福感带来的负面影响。

(2)政府在履行管理与服务职能时应学习中国传统文化中的先进理念。坚持"以民为本"、"恤民为德"的原则,真正做到为人民谋福利,为国民求幸福;继承"小康大同"的社会理想,努力缩小贫富差距,并建立惠及全体国民的分配制度;构建"礼之用,和为贵"的和谐社会秩序及平等公正的社会氛围;在全社会宣扬并引导民众学习传统文化精髓,彻底摒弃文化糟粕,如"等级尊卑"和"奴性文化",这些思想牺牲了独立精神和自我人格,不利于当今平等风气的形成和社会公正的完全实现,更不利于国民幸福感的培养和提升。

(3)在全球化浪潮带来思想多元化的背景下,政府应适度放开文化限制并引导一种平等、自由、开放的文化氛围,宣扬积极乐观精神,使人们能够平等和谐相处、乐观积极并对未来充满希望。另外,政府应大力发展文化产业和文化事业,同时创新文化引导机制,增强文化潜移默化的感染力。

参 考 文 献

Alesina,A. Di,Tella,R. & MacCulloch,R. 2004. Inequality and happiness：Are European and Americans different? *Journal of Public Economics*,88(9):2009 - 2042.

Arrindell, W. A. , Hatzichristou, C. , Wensink, J. , Rosenberg, E. , van Twillert, B. & Stedema, J. 1997. Dimensions of national culture as predictors of cross - national differences in subjective well - being. *Personality and Individual Differences*,23(1): 37 - 53.

Brockmann,H. ,Delhey,J. ,Welzel,C. & Hao Y. 2008. The China puzzle：Falling happiness in a rising economy. *Journal of Happiness Studies*,10(4):387 - 405.

Chui,A. & Kwok,C. 2008. National culture and life insurance consumption. *Journal of International Business Studie*,39(1):88 - 101.

Ye, D. Yew - Kwang Ng & Lian, Y. 2014. *Culture and Happiness*. Soc Indic Res, 10: 205 - 214.

Easterlin,R. A. 1995. Will raising the incomes of all increase the happiness of all? *Journal of Economic Behavior and Organization*,27(1):35 - 47.

Graham,C. & Pettinato,S. 2006. Happiness, markets and democracy：Latin American in comparative perspective. *Journal of Happiness Studies*,2(3):237 - 268.

Hargerty,M. 2000. Social comparisons of income in one's community：Evidence from national survey of income and happiness. *Journal of Personality and Social Psychology*, 78(4):764 - 771.

Luttmer,E. 2004. Neighbors as negatives：Relative earnings and well - being. *Quarterly Journal of Economics*,120(3):963 - 1002.

Marks,H. R. & Kitayama,S. 1998. *Emotion and Culture：Empirical Studies of Mutual Infuence*. Washington,DC：American Psychological Association,89 - 130.

Morawetz,D. 1997. Income distrubition and self - rated happiness：Some empirical evidence. *Economic Journal*,347:511 - 522.

Oshio,T. & Kobayash,M. 2011. Area - level income inequality and individual happiness：Evidence from Japan. *Journal of Happiness Studies*,12(4):633 - 649.

Thompson,R. W. & Roper,R. E. 2011. *Relative Deprivation in Buganda：The Relation of Wealth,Security,and Opportunity to the Perception of Economic Satisfaction*. American Anthropological Association,4:155 - 187.

Stutzer,A. & Frey,B. S. 2006. Does marriage make people happy, or do happy people get married? *The Journal of Socio - Economics*,35:326 - 347.

何立新,潘春阳. 2007. 破解中国的 Easterlin 悖论：收入差距、机会不均与居民幸福感. 管理世界,(8):11 - 22.

陆洛. 2007. 华人的幸福观与幸福感. 心理学应用探索,(9):19 - 30.

袁正,郑欢,韩骁. 2013. 收入水平、分配公平与幸福感. 当代财经,(10):5 - 11.

王淑燕,奚彦．2008．主观幸福感研究述评——基于个体主义—集体主义文化．心理研究,(5):42－46.

张学志,才国伟．2011．收入、价值观与居民幸福感——来自广东成人调查数据的经验证据．管理世界,(9):63－73.

《跨文化管理》投稿须知

Call for Papers
Cross - Cultural Management

　　《跨文化管理》集刊(*Cross - Cultural Management*)是上海外国语大学国际工商管理学院主办,由经济管理出版社出版的前沿性跨文化管理学术集刊,暂定每年2辑。它以推进跨文化管理学的学术和应用研究水平、介绍该领域国内外研究的最新进展以及加强国内外学者和研究机构之间的交流为宗旨。

　　《跨文化管理》集刊发表原创性的关于跨文化管理以及相关领域的理论、实证和综述性研究论文。国内外公开征文。相关内容可涉及:比较管理学与跨文化管理、东方管理与东西方管理比较、跨国经营与跨文化管理、跨文化职能管理、跨文化与无国界领导力开发、跨文化公共事务管理案例、跨文化产业与企业管理案例、跨文化管理学术资讯等。集刊采用国际通告的匿名审稿制,倡导独立、客观的研究和严谨、规范的研究方法,提倡和促进学术观点的交流与探讨。

　　《跨文化管理》集刊投稿以中文为主,也可用英文投稿,但必须是未发表的稿件。

　　《跨文化管理》集刊采用国际通行的注释体例,编辑部将在收到投稿后,当即向作者回函确认,并在三个月内答复作者是录用、修改后再投还是不予录用,初审通过将请作者惠发电子版。因工作量大,所赐稿件恕不退还,请作者自留底稿。参考文献及注释规范请以本论文集为标准。

　　诚邀海内外管理学界的专家学者踊跃投稿!

　　《跨文化管理》各卷将陆续推出,欢迎海内外学者将自己的跨文化管理学研究成果邮寄至(或电邮至)上海外国语大学国际工商管理学院,具体联络方式为:

　　上海市大连西路550号1号楼316室

　　上海外国语大学国际工商管理学院

　　《跨文化管理》编辑部收

　　邮编:200083

　　电子邮箱:ccccib@163.com

　　电话:86 - 021 - 35372663

　　传真:86 - 021 - 35372940

　　(请注明《跨文化管理》编辑部收)

图书在版编目 (CIP) 数据

跨文化管理. 第 7 辑/上海外国语大学国际工商管理学院主编. —北京:经济管理出版社,2017.6

ISBN 978 – 7 – 5096 – 5180 – 3

Ⅰ. ①跨…　Ⅱ. ①上…　Ⅲ. ①企业文化—跨文化管理—丛刊　Ⅳ. ①F270 – 55

中国版本图书馆 CIP 数据核字(2017)第 135871 号

组稿编辑：申桂萍
责任编辑：侯春霞
责任印制：黄章平
责任校对：赵天宇

出版发行：经济管理出版社
　　　　　（北京市海淀区北蜂窝 8 号中雅大厦 A 座 11 层　100038）
网　　　址：http://www. E – mp. com. cn
电　　　话：(010) 51915602
印　　　刷：玉田县昊达印刷有限公司
经　　　销：新华书店
开　　　本：720mm×1000mm/16
印　　　张：10. 25
字　　　数：184 千字
版　　　次：2017 年 6 月第 1 版　　2017 年 6 月第 1 次印刷
书　　　号：ISBN 978 – 7 – 5096 – 5180 – 3
定　　　价：48. 00 元